D1286903

EDUCATING

EDUCATING

D. Bob Gowin

Cornell University Press

ITHACA AND LONDON

First published 1981 by Cornell University Press.
Published in the United Kingdom by Cornell University Press Ltd.,
Ely House, 37 Dover Street, London W1X 4HQ

International Standard Book Number 0-8014-1418-0
Library of Congress Catalog Card Number 81-66646
Printed in the United States of America
Librarians: Library of Congress cataloging information appears on the last page of the book.

To my friends, students, teachers,
often the same people

Contents

	Preface	9
	Acknowledgments	19
ONE.	Studying Educating	23
TWO.	A Theory of Educating	35
THREE.	Teaching	62
FOUR.	Curriculum	84
FIVE.	Learning	122
SIX.	Governance	153
SEVEN.	Self-Educating: Ends and Endings	195
	Bibliography	203
	Index	207

Preface

In America, schooling has been recognized as a route to success. According to Christopher Jencks (1979), completing high school raises earnings only modestly, but completing college raises them more substantially. You must go to school to get ahead. You have no choice but to want to get ahead and be successful. For hundreds of thousands of people since the invention of the American high school in the early part of the twentieth century, these rules have put gold in pockets. The longer you stay in school, the more money you will make in your lifetime—so goes one line of the Success Doctrine. As events and thus the facts change, however, this dominant doctrine loses force. At a time when upward of 80 to 85 percent of age cohorts graduate from high school—that is, at a time when nearly everybody has the same credential—the value of that credential to differentiate individuals reduces to almost zero. What everybody has is not valued in a marketplace governed by scarcity and specialization. The old glitter has gone. A new justification for schooling is sorely needed.

There are other serious problems in contemporary schooling. In March, 1960, Project TALENT, funded by the United States Office of Education and directed by John C. Flanagan, began to collect data from 40,000 high school students in the United States. In 1975, 1,000 of the original participants were selected for follow-up interviews. Writing of Project TALENT, philosopher Michael Scriven claims "that this best of all studies of our educational system tells a sorry story of our schools. The story it tells is one of education for non-citizenship, of education for apathy." Psychologist Robert Gagné, appraising the contribution of schooling to occupation, family life, citizenship, and life enjoyment, concludes that traditional high school education serves no very useful purpose for the majority of the people. Educator Ralph Tyler notes that subjects taught for purposes of "general education are not achieving their aims for students." Measurement expert Gene Glass writes that "schools could do a better job of helping children become literate and employable adults . . . [but] they are accomplishing almost nothing toward achieving the goals of helping children to develop emotional maturity, understanding, and acceptance of self and others, and the ability to form satisfying relationships." Glass notes that measurement and documentation of problems in education are a prerequisite to any possible improvement. (Flanagan 1979: 76, 35, 45–46, 69.)

School reform will not emerge simply from documenting the problems of schools; however, until we properly understand the phenomena of educating, we will never understand how to reform schooling. Educating itself, in the argument of this book, is what we should be studying. Yet when we begin to study it, we almost immediately run into peculiar and puzzling problems requiring a new conceptualization.

Educating and its more frequently experienced stand-in, miseducating, are universal phenomena required for cultural continuity. Older generations educate oncoming generations. The phenomena of educating require change (for example, from immaturity to maturity, from ignorance to knowledge), and because they require change, I choose to focus on educative events, supported in part by an assumption of modern process philosophy, that all existents are events. Educating is a social event of sharing meanings. The fact that meanings can be shared between individual persons makes the events of educating possible.

The conditions of shared meaning in the context of educating have patterns, and thus the events can be subjected to rational (planned) inquiry, even though the regularities are artifactual (not natural). Making educative events happen is a consequence of human choice, invention, and inauguration. Literally thousands of educative events happen. Believing that we should seek simplicity, but preserve complexity, I have found most congenial the four commonplaces of education—teaching, curriculum, learning, social milieu. I accept Joseph J. Schwab's (1978) view that these four commonplaces are both incommensurable and of equal weight. That means to me that we should not try to reduce them to one, as is often done by psychologists who study only the phenomena of learning, thinking that if we understood it, we would know what to do in teaching. Learning, in the context of educating, is very unlike what most psychologists study in their isolating, narrowing experimental settings. Since the student should be free to choose to learn, the efficient cause of learning is the learner. This means, in part, that the responsibility for learning is also the learner's (not the teacher's).

The curriculum stands separately, also, as an object of inquiry. I use epistemology as a way to think about knowledge and the curriculum. Knowledge about knowledge is the guide to curriculum inquiry. The curriculum is an analyzed record of prior events which we use to make new events happen; the curriculum is to be related to teaching and to learning, but not reduced to either.

The social milieu is a powerful set of forces governing education. To take account of these conditions I use concepts from ethics and social philosophy—equality, freedom, authority, mutuality, social justice. And I center on the problems of governance (social control) in making educative events happen. Each of the four commonplaces gets separate analysis but always with a concern for how each commonplace relates to the others.

Actions, not simple behaviors, concern me, because I think actions are behaviors with meanings. I believe educating helps people come into conscious possession of their powers (and their own world), especially the flourishing integration of thinking and feeling and acting. As educative events come more and more under the control of individuals, educating becomes self-educating. And that is the end of education (pun intended).

The key concepts—events, experience, change, choice, meaning (both grasped and shared), claims (both knowledge and value claims), criteria of excellence, and so forth—are related definitionally to the central notion of meaning. A logically consistent set of related terms and distinctions pointing toward regularities in educative events is the idea of theory I use.

Educating is a complex undertaking. Schooling is also complex, but the overlap and coincidence between educating and schooling are highly various. One is not the cause of the other, though they may coexist. One is not necessary to the other, though they seem mutually dependent. One is not the aim of the other, though they may share means. And one is not the product of the other, even though the process of educating can be common to both.

To sort out the claims of these complex events of educating and schooling will be difficult. Very likely we will need to step back from our immediate involvement in such practical activities as teaching, curriculum-making, administration, evaluating, and so forth, in order to gain perspective. We need a new pair of spectacles—conceptual goggles—in order to see the practical spectacle of educative events. In short, we need a new theory of educating.

Recently I gave a lecture on some of the ideas in this book to a group of graduate students and faculty members of the University of Chicago's Department of Education. The exchange was vigorous, critical, and wide-ranging. Almost at the end of the three-hour discussion one student attempted to summarize his understanding. He asked, "You seem to be saying that we need a theory of educating in order to study educating. Right? You criticize theories from psychology and sociology as inappropriate for the study of education. Right? You think we should be constructing conceptualizations of the phenomena of educating, that we need a theory, right?"

I responded, "Right. We do need a theory of educating."

In developing a theory I draw upon philosophical studies of educating and scientific research, but I recognize that such studies very often fail to make sense of ordinary educative events. We need a special theory of educating to increase our understanding. This book moves in that direction by offering a framework of ideas for conceptualizing phenomena of education.

Education, a social institution and personal achievement, remains perplexingly opaque to scholarly study. We do not seem to be improving our intelligence about it, in spite of hundreds (even thousands) of empirical studies. Why? The baleful influence of a positivistic approach to science with its disastrous separation of fact and value has been significantly misleading. Research methodologies that move away from instead of into studies of educative events have contributed their share to misplaced claims. The work of philosophic analysts has seldom been directed specifically to the difficulties of research practice. The Dewey legacy—a belief that intelligent science will reconstruct social and moral matters—has not delivered on its promise to education.

Are educative events distinctive? How are these phenomena to be conceptualized? To study educating is to become intelligent about becoming intelligent. What intellectual tasks confront us as we seek to achieve this aim?

The general answer is that we need a conceptualization appropriate to the events of interest. Normal science is not appropriate because the regularities of educating are artifactual (cultural), not natural. The standard philosophies of science do not provide theories of education that stimulate actual inquiry into educational phenomena. Common sense and the conventional wisdom about the practice of educating sometimes lead us closer to educative events, but the concepts are richly ambiguous and the facts severely partial. Nevertheless, from the recorded efforts of science, philosophy, and common sense, we *can* forge a theory of educating that will bring together facts, concepts, and events. By centering our attention on the four commonplaces of educating—teacher, learner, curriculum, and governance—we will come to understand educating as an eventful process.

One of the basic expectations of education is a preparation for adult life. A major social function of schooling is vocational: to help young people find their way into jobs and occupations and work. Moreover, we can look at school work as the main job of the pupil. When we take this point of view, we see both positive and negative similarities between schooling and working. On the positive side, schooling sometimes actually leads a pupil to find a "life work," a calling. When this is the outcome, we are usually very pleased. On the negative side, however, we find schooling to be a preparation for working primarily because pupils learn to persist at largely routine and meaningless tasks in schools to find, unfortunately, that working at most jobs consists of the same thing: routine, boring, and life-defeating activities.

Consider the first sentences of Louis Terkel's *Working* (1972):

> This book, being about work, is, by its very nature, about violence—to the spirit as well as to the body. . . . It is, above all (or beneath all), about daily humiliations. To survive the day is triumph enough for the walking wounded among the great many of us. . . . It is about a search, too, for daily meaning as well as daily bread, for recognition as well as cash, for astonishment rather than torpor; in short, for a sort of life rather than a Monday through Friday sort of dying.

Why is it that work is so closely related to violence? Why do schools become so readily associated with humiliation and aggression? Must unpleasant experience be associated with educating? How can we account for violence to the body and mind and spirit?

It seems true that forms of symbolic violence often occur unintentionally. For example, a person confronted with powerful new ideas can feel ignorant, even humiliated and terrified. The new often combines feelings in us of terror and titillation, of fear and the promise of freedom. The dialectic between where we are when we start to learn and when we finish causes us to endure certain oppressions because they are thought necessary to desirable liberation. That condition often obscures the promise of educating.

Educating is demeaning, and necessarily so, but with an ever-present option of liberation from oppression. If we are in a state of ignorance of what some authority knows to be right, good, true, beautiful, and complexly powerful, we may feel an oppressive gap between our ignorance and the authority's knowledge. Feeling impressed by authority and depressed by ignorance sets the stage for oppression: the unjust or cruel exercise of authority. Nor does the oppression have to come from the outside; we can impose burdens on ourselves when we set out to master new areas of knowledge. Ignorance is not such a bad thing, however, and seen in the right light can become a positive quality. Plato, aging, writing *The Republic,* tells us that he no longer believes evil to be the result of ignorance (since no one knowingly does harm); evil is the result of knowledge powerfully placed in the hands of the arrogant and unjust.

Because ignorance is a necessary precondition of knowledge, just as immaturity is a prior condition of maturity, both therefore need not be negative qualities, even though the practices of schooling and educating often treat them negatively. Educating, in turn, need not be oppressive, though it often is, and even in the best cases some burden is to be expected; suppression of some normal and natural expressions is inevitable because no one can focus on everything at once. Educating, and becoming educated, can lead through an educative process properly governed to knowledge, power, and great human value if the process can run its full course.

Having suggested that violence is associated with schooling and that terror stalks ignorance, it is good to suggest also that exhilaration and titillation accompany grasping the meaning of something so new as to promise a change in the meaning of our experience. Consider D. H. Lawrence's description, in *The Rainbow,* of young Ursula, living in the beginning of this century:

> Ursula seated herself upon the hill of learning, looking down on the smoke and confusion and the manufacturing, engrossed activity of the town. She was happy. Up here, in the Grammar School, she fancied the air was finer, beyond the factory smoke. She wanted to learn Latin and Greek and French and mathematics. She trembled like a postulant when she wrote the Greek alphabet for the first time.
>
> She was upon another hill-slope, whose summit she had not scaled. There was always the marvellous eagerness in her heart, to climb and to see beyond. A Latin verb was virgin soil to her: she sniffed a new odour in it; it meant something, though she did not know what it meant. But she gathered it up: it was significant. When she knew that
>
> $$x^2 - y^2 = (x + y)(x - y)$$
>
> then she felt that she had grasped something, that she was liber-

> ated into an intoxicating air, rare and unconditioned. And she was very glad as she wrote her French exercise:
>
> "J'ai donné le pain à mon petit frère."
>
> In all these things there was the sound of a bugle to her heart, exhilarating, summoning her to perfect places. She never forgot her brown "Longman's First French Grammar," nor her "Via Latina" with its red edges, nor her little grey Algebra book. There was always magic in them.

The needed new justification for schooling is an old one: to make schools places where educating occurs. At the present time schooling is not educating. It is serving many social utilities at the expense of utilities for educating. The modern curriculum may be more than the French, Latin, and algebra that excited Ursula, but the balance between terror and titillation should be present. Educating reduces boredom, enhances living, changes the meaning of human experience.

The formulation of a theory of educating encourages a solution to the classic theory-practice problem. Both researchers and practitioners should find the theory useful. Both parties are concerned with educative events, and the theory is a guide to thinking (and feeling and acting) about these events. Some readers may find this book a descriptive phenomenology, and the focus on events of educating is deliberate. But it is also a conceptualization and an idealization going beyond a mere description of what exists. The theory can be taken also as a normative construction, suggesting what ought to be and why. As a theory it should be tested through practice and research.

Some research using the theory has already been completed (Gowin 1981). Educative events—ephemeral, episodic—are hard to study because facts about them, as records of events, are difficult to establish. We have used videotapes, audiotapes, semi-clinical interviews with children, older students, teachers, and college populations in our studies. College and university teaching, curriculum, learning, and governance have been major focuses. Concept-mapping techniques have been tested out with children of all ages and found useful. Studies have been completed in physics (optics), educational research, English literature (short stories), linguistics (second-language instruction), mathematics (calculus), earth science and ecology (elementary school), biology (junior and senior high school), chemistry (high school and college). A program of research at Cornell University is growing with these various uses of the theory. Much remains to be done to study the complex phenomena of educating. It is my belief that needed school reforms require improvements in our understanding of educating itself.

My hope is to present in this book a rounded view of many matters educated people work with and worry about, beginning in midstream. Just as writing is always rewriting, educating is reeducating. It is a continual process of working and reworking, structuring and restructuring the qualities of human experience interacting with nature.

D. Bob Gowin

Ithaca, New York

Acknowledgments

Many people have helped me to shape the concepts and facts of this book. No one of them has seen the completed work; I hope that when they do they will understand their roles in educating me. I have been cordially welcomed into their places of life and work, sharing meaning, learning, teaching. To them all, I say many thanks: SUNY at Albany: Mark Berger, Mauritz Johnson, Dorothy McClellan, James McClellan; University of Buffalo: David Nyberg, Michael Simmons; University of Chicago: Harold Dunkel, Jo Jackson, Philip Jackson, Joseph Schwab; Cornell University: Max Black, David Henderson, Donald Holcomb, James Maas, Jay Millman, James Noblitt, George Posner, Walter Slatoff, Frederick Stutz, Nevart Yaghlian; University of Delaware: Jane Friedman, Martin Friedman, James Hawk, Jon Magoon; Simon Fraser University: Kieran Egan, Susanna Egan; Florida State University: Eugene Kaelin, James Macmillan, Sande Milton, Emanuel Shargel, Mia Shargel; University of Illinois: Harry Broudy, Jack Easley, Robert Stake, Patricia Templin; Michigan State University: Lee Shulman; Northwest Regional Educational Laboratory: Darrell Cauley, Nick L. Smith; Ohio State University: Richard Pratte, Gerald Reagan; University of Pennsylvania: Charles Dwyer; Pennsylvania State University: Harold Mitzel, Edmund Short; Stanford University: Lee Cronbach, Elliot Eisner, Evelyn Thomas, Lawrence Thomas, Decker Walker; in Sweden: Urban Dahloff, Daniel Kallos, Ulf Lundgren; Syracuse University: Rosemary

Green, Thomas F. Green, Emily Haynes, Judith Long Laws; Virginia Polytechnic Institute: Gary Fenstermacher, Sheila Slaughter; Washington University: Barry Anderson, Bryce Hudgins, Louis Smith, Alan Tom, Arthur Wirth; Yale University: John Brubacher, Clyde Hill, Mark A. May.

In the actual production of a readable manuscript, I received great help from Lynda Farrar, Doreet Hopp, Sidney Siskin, and Marj Hulin Young, and I thank them heartily.

I appreciate the personal support I have received from Laura Gowin Seitz, Marie Betts Gowin, Sarah Gowin, Robin Gowin, John Gowin, and Laura Levine.

Thanks, too, go to generations of Cornell students who have tested some of these ideas in their theses and dissertations: Joshua Aisiku (teacher education), Amos Akingba (economic development), Charles Ault (earth science), Chris Bogden (genetics), Bernardo Buchweitz (optics), Peter Cardamone (mathematics), Hai Chen (laboratory chemistry), Lynne DeJonghe (child psychology), Ann Dyckman (piano pedagogy), Lynda Farrar (linguistics), Doreet Hopp (English short stories), Roger Johansen (math), William Kelley (biblical literature), June Kinigstein (ecology), Richard Mitchell (prison education), Francesca Mollura (physiology), Marco Moreira (physics), Marli Moreira (poetry), Leon Pines (scientific concept learning in children), Frances Rosamond (mathematics), James Stewart (biology), Margaret Somers (English composition), David Taylor-Way (video-tape recall), Margaret Waterman (plant physiology), and Daniel P. Wood (sports education). These students have often surprised me by their connection and extension of meaning into fields where I have little knowledge. Professor Joseph Novak and I have co-sponsored much of their work, and I am most grateful to him for his intelligent and unfailing support of all of us.

The Department of Education and Cornell University through their enlightened principles of educational governance have contributed much to my work.

D.B.G.

EDUCATING

CHAPTER ONE

Studying Educating

Begin in midstream. Begin with persons who are already educated to some extent. Neither educating nor the study of educating begins with a blank slate, a clear page, undisturbed phenomena. Students, even young ones, already know a lot when schooling begins (Donaldson 1978). They have fears, joys, loves, passions, depressions. They think, feel, and act. Educating these individuals will, from now on, be reeducating: reconstructing what they already know and value into new patterns. Formal schooling begins in midstream because by the time youngsters come to school, they already have a language, a cluster of concepts, a set of facts and habits of conduct to manage their lives with some competence (Matthews 1980).

Basic Difficulties

Self-Reflexive Phenomena of Interest

Schooling, in the early years, regards students as persons who should be able to make objects of themselves. They learn to treat themselves as objects, because this helps them to learn about learning to learn: they learn to see, do, think, and feel about themselves in the context of learning. Each of us finds out, at some time in life, just how we learn; and if we are efficient, we use this knowledge of our personal ways of learning to help us develop knowledge of other things. We draw our own "epistemic self-portrait" (Toulmin 1972). This knowledge about knowledge, or learning about learning, is a significant fact for those who would study educating. For those people are, among other things, learning about how others learn about learning—three layers of learning—and you can add a fourth for the researcher who thinks about learning about learning to learn. Thus we come to the first peculiar and perplexingly difficulty basic to the study of educating—its phenomena are layered, reflexive, self-inspecting, as subjects become objects.

How can we think and write about these complex phenomena without becoming either bogged down in the ambiguities of the language of education or overcome by the complexities of the specific content of the thousands of occasions of educating? We can begin by citing clear cases of educating. Of these clear cases (and perhaps later some counterexamples) we can begin to search for patterns, commonalities.

Consider these cases:

A coach and a player going over a playbook together; an editor and a writer sharing a manuscript; a parent and a child reading instructions to assemble a three-wheel tractor from a box; an architect and a builder studying blueprints for a building; a scientist and a technician making records of an event in an experiment; a teacher and a pupil reading a poem over several times together; a cook and a helper discussing four different recipes for roast goose; a journalist and a policeman reviewing the facts of a case; a carpenter and a home-owner planning a garage; an orchestra conductor and the trumpet section interpreting passages of a musical score; a doctor and a nurse reviewing a case history.

On these occasions human beings are sharing ideas and documents as a way to make sense of human experience and nature. Both parties to the exchange grasp the meaning the material carries as the basis for the mutual understanding. Each of these human practices develops its own language, a set of meanings and distinctions often codelike in brevity; of each of these pairs of persons, the one who uses the document to help the other understand it is the teacher. The student is the one who needs the teacher to "crack the code." In all cases the document is a record of some prior happening (event), a record used as a guide to making subsequent events happen. These documented claims are the curriculum.

Next we must note that these exchanges take place in a social context. Just the fact of language is enough to indicate that. When we add the joining together of two persons over a document, we have further indications of a social context, for each must take the actions of the other as a basis for further action of the self. The social context can be open or closed, liberating or oppressive, demeaning or mutually supportive, but whatever the quality of the social order, some quality will be found there and will serve to mark off one situation from another. Getting things done in a social context requires administration.

We have now touched on the major commonplaces in educating (teacher, curriculum, students, and governing social order) that are common to the highly diverse and complex events of human life which are educative events. To study educating is to become intelligent about educating. How can we do so? Very likely in no way substantially different from getting smart about anything else—by study, experience, reflection, action, more study, and so forth. Why don't we get smart?

Embedded Familiarity

There is a catch here. If we are becoming more intelligent about genetics or poetry or life insurance, we are being educated in these matters. A more intelligent geneticist is not necessarily more intelligent about educating. The catch is that becoming more intelligent about anything that matters to us does not in itself also make us more intelligent about how we got that way. We are *in* the process but not above it, studying it, noting its peculiar features and unique difficulties. It takes a special effort to detach ourselves sufficiently to study educating and to reattach ourselves to the common human activity of becoming educated. When Freud "discovered" that day dreams and night dreams take up half our life, he was like a dolphin genius discovering water. What is so much around and in us is too close and too familiar for us to see clearly. It is like tasting our tongue; it is there all along but we do not notice it. Because the process of educating is so familiar yet so complex, we will need a way to achieve perspective. We may need a new and perhaps strange vocabulary and conceptual scheme. We need a linguistic shock to our common experience to avoid the clichés of conventional wisdom. We risk banality in studying what is common in educative events. We risk bloodless abstraction in conceptualizing these events. We risk the quest for certainty in making affirmative claims. But these risks must be taken to provide a theory of educating that will guide the study of educating.

It is not so obvious as it seems at first thought that we need a theory, and why we need one. If it were obvious, then theory-making would be more common. I suspect the difficulty here is to be found in inappropriate conceptions of theory itself.

The notion of theory consists of many different views of theory. It is important not to be misled by the uncritical adoption of the standard, or currently preferred, notion of theory. Of the most common notions of theory none really serves our purpose well. The theory we need should be an organized set of concepts signifying regularities in distinctively educative events, and these events should be susceptible to being recorded. That is, we need a theory that will join concepts, events, and facts intelligibly.

Mutable, Artifactual Phenomena of Interest

Educative events are formed by human agents; they are inventions; they are social constructions; their realities vary as their constructions vary. Every culture, if it is to continue, must form patterns for the education of oncoming generations.

Educative events are artifactual, not natural, mutable not immutable. Although they occur as a matter of course in human experience (and thus appear natural, i.e., common, familiar), they are brought about by human beings. These artifactual phenomena are culture patterns and not the invariant sequences of nature reported by an abstract science (like physics). If, for example, some cultural pattern is studied by social scientists and some claims to contribution of knowledge result, it is possible for human beings who use this knowledge to change the social conditions so that the original claims no longer hold true. Claims to knowledge are discardable, perishable, consumed in the progress of understanding.

Let us take a clear case. If studies of sexism in American culture result in claims that education in elementary schools helps to form stereotypes of sex roles, then conditions can be changed and the original claims will no longer be valid. We do know, in fact, that sex-role stereotyping occurs early in elementary school education. Around 1970 educators, stimulated by feminists, began to sharpen their awareness of the sexism in school textbooks. As a consequence, text materials were rewritten, publishers cooperated, books were revised, and educational practices changed. Ten years later the claims of 1970 are no longer true. Those knowledge claims have been used to indicate changes in practice: the use of true claims results in their falsification when conditions change.

The phenomena of interest in research on education are mutable because they are products of deliberate choice and deliberate acting. Such choosing and acting presupposes that the phenomena of interest are capable of being changed, since deliberation itself presupposes that things could be otherwise. Now let us suppose that the phenomena are immutable. One aim of science is to discover laws based on unchanging regularities in the events of the universe. This Aristotelian aim of theoretic science is a poor choice for researchers on education, because the phenomena of interest in education are changing rather than inevitably uniform. Education research must construct an aim of research that is fitting to the phenomena of interest. There *are* regularities in educational phenomena; the researcher should not give up searching for them and should back assertions about them with well-chosen evidence. To these regularities I attach the qualifier that they are artifactual. I use the word to contrast with the phrase "events given in nature," or the universe, which events can be aptly described by statements (propositions, theories) in the form of laws.

Claims of knowledge are perishable. More durable, however, is knowledge about knowledge (see below, Chapter 4). The structure of knowledge is a basic concern in educating, seen most clearly in the curriculum. All knowledge, a deliberate construction of human beings striving to know about nature and experience, has structure. We know this about knowledge because we can analyze constructed claims of knowledge. We can see what elements have to be brought together to make a structure. These elements (for example, theory, facts, assertions, assumptions, etc.) may vary in their roles and intensities in any particular set of knowledge claims. But some version of the key elements will always be present. One only has to provide an analysis of any purported set of such claims to see this structure. Thus whatever we know about the structure of knowledge we can easily see is knowledge of another sort, knowledge about knowledge. And this kind of knowledge is more durable than any particular set of knowledge claims, some of which are consumed, made out of date, by the progressive ordering of new knowledge.

A Way Out

We do need a theory of educating. A theory of educating can be constructed, but it will have to be a theory in the *wide* sense of scientific theory. A theory of educating will help make sense of educative events. The key event is *a teacher teaching meaningful materials to a student who grasps the meaning of the materials under humane conditions of social control.* The teacher initiates the event, the materials (curriculum) are guides to the event, the students take part in the event, the event as a social event has distinctive qualities governing it. We have, again, four commonplaces: teacher, curriculum, learner, governance.

These four commonplaces are our phenomena of interest. We can characterize them differently as we build theories of education, but we cannot do without explicit reference to some concept of each of them, some account of how they relate to one another, nor can we avoid making records of events as they take place. Thus we need to be clear about events, concepts, and records of events as they take place.

An Event Epistemology

Imagine a large letter V (see Chapter 4). The bottom of the V points toward the events we want to study. Either we make records of these events (as experimenters do) or we study records already made (as historians do). These records I call *facts.* To talk about facts is to talk about three related things: the event, the record, and the judgment that the record is indeed the record of the event it purports to be a record of. As I move up the right hand side of the imagined V (as I study records), I begin to transform these facts. I begin to order the facts by ranking, by drawing graphs, by making tables, by making categories. When I assign a name or a number to a record of an event according to a rule, I am engaged in quantification and measurement. When I put measurements into statistical models, I transform them. These transformed facts I call *data.* It is always important not to lose the thread of meaning that facts have as a consequence of statistical manipulation of data.

As I move up the left-hand side of the V, I come to *concepts.* A concept is a sign/symbol pointing toward regularities in events, or to records of events. Concepts are usually words, terms, ingredients in sentences and propositions. They may be number concepts, of course, or concepts carried by other symbols (such as musical notations). But the key thing about concepts is their office of signifying regularities. Concepts are centrally important to us because people think with concepts.

Basic Requirements

The first thing to be concerned with is also the last thing. We must first identify some event that we are willing to call an "educative event." Begin with a clear case (above, p. 24). All that is required is that at least three competent educators agree that the event, in its *wholeness,* is indeed an educative event.

Then find a way to make a record of the event. I like to make videotapes of episodes of college teaching. Whatever way is used, the record of the educative event must be reliable—that is, we must be assured that it is the record that it purports to be, that we can get other judges to read it, and that we can repeatedly study it from different points of view. Replaying videotapes settles the question of the repeatability of the record. Do not forget, however, that the criterion of validity has already been satisfied: the event has already been judged by competent judges to be an educative event, although their criteria for so judging have yet to be made explicit. That validity comes before reliability is a reversal of the order of standard research recommendations.

Next, find a way to make sense of the event. We can ask ourselves, "What's going on here?" Is someone teaching? Is some person learning? Is some claim of knowledge being asserted? Is the process governed by humane and reasonable rules such that it is likely that a person might sensibly grasp the meaning of the material the teacher presents? These are easy questions for experienced educators to *ask;* what is not so easy is to realize that embedded in them are key concepts: of teaching, of learning, of knowledge, of governance. What do we mean by these concepts? How are we to define them? At this point our competent judges will begin to disagree, to find fault, to hedge their bets, to qualify, to waffle, to wish (which is not possible, if we are to do research), to change the subject. We must stick to the example. We must make our concepts clear in terms that identify some part of the events as the teaching part, if that is the concept we use—or the learning part, if *that* is the part we use, or the knowledge claim or the governance part. In brief, tie your key concept to the particular part of the record of the event which you call a fact. To isolate from the complex event one part that exhibits a regularity is to define the concept you are using. You may wish to change the concepts when the concept does not fit the facts, but that is all right. It may be called "concept improvement." To use facts to improve concepts is another significant change in recommendations of standard research.

Once the concepts you think with have been defined, try to make some order out of the facts. Here again there are many gambits in standard procedures of education research as they are commonly understood. Make tables. Draw graphs. Whenever you can, count. Assign numbers to events according to a rule—that is, measure. Rank, Rate. Correlate. Analyze and synthesize. In short, compose a set of statements about the record in some form, be it a paragraph or a paradigm sketch, which consist of a set of summary judgments of the facts. These are *factual judgments.* The judgment part comes in when we order the facts and thereby judge their merit according to some criterion of significance. Notice that in the category of facts are included these items in relation: the event itself (which either is made to happen or just happens), the record of the event, and the factual (including moral) judgments based on the record. It is easy to make mistakes at each of these places, so we need reliability checks at each place. Notice another difference from standard research ideas: the usual tables, charts, graphs, etc., which fill our journals are not facts in either of the first two senses (events, record). These journals are filled with factual judgments two steps removed from the events of interest.

Now back to thinking. Interpretation consists of thinking about knowledge claims with substantive concepts of educating. That is, we can now ask a variety of new questions about the meaning of the data we have gathered, the claims we have made. Furthermore, now that we have gone back to thinking, we can redefine some of our key concepts. We can import, for example, a different concept of teaching and see if the new concept is supported. Or see if the new concept gives a new ordering to the factual judgments. Or see if we need to invent a new concept in order to account for some perceived regularity. Sometimes this rethinking process is called "rehashing the data" to try to make it come out right. But it sounds to me more like rethinking the concepts than rehashing the data. At this point Conant's maxim (borrowed from Bridgman) for science is apt: do your damnedest with your mind with no holds barred! We are, after all, doing something when we think in a disciplined way. Doing research is not merely gathering data. It is gathering thoughts as well. There is a radically different set of skills needed for concept analysis, concept improvement, concept definition than is needed for fact-making. A most common mistake books on education research make is to omit materials on the methods and techniques of concept analysis. Statistical analysis is not concept analysis; it is *data* analysis.

I do not mean to suggest that the five basic requirements are to be followed through a fixed chronological sequence. Moreover, thinking can take place before and after each step, and as a result one can begin by clarifying the concepts or by ordering the facts, and so forth.

Concepts of education and concept analysis are the substance and method of the philosophy of education. Research methodologists have difficulty seeing that philosophizing is a method of work. Some research methodologists have produced brilliant works much more like philosophy in substance and method than like empirical research. Some philosophers, likewise, have engaged in studies very close to what really happens in significant educative events. But these occasional mutants survive in the side waters of the conceptual pool.

A Method of Study

Disciplined criticism of previous studies of educational phenomena of interest is the general method used to generate the theory of educating presented here. In brief, this approach consists of careful study of and reflection about what has been produced by others. It is like the attempt to understand art by studying what artists produce. It is like trying to comprehend science by analyzing the products of technology. The starting point consists of exemplar products—which, our mythical three educational experts would agree initially, are examples of educational products.

Plato, Aristotle, Rousseau, and Dewey, among others, have created for the Western world statements about education that make sense (Ulich 1948; Nakosteen 1965). Their views, and variants of their views, are all around us now, buried in our language, objectified in our school buildings, made into scripts and slogans uttered at ritual celebrations of educational practice. Characteristically, this type of theory is ideological, or normative, constructed out of social claims by philosophical methods of work.

Protagoras and the Sophists, Comenius and other Protestants, August Hermann Francke and the Realschule of real things, Pestalozzi and the object method of instruction, Froebel and the kindergarten, Herbart, Tolstoy, Montessori, A. S. Neill, and many, many others have left a deposit of documents about education which are a result of the conscious move from philosophical doctrines to educational practices. Making man the measure of all things meant you could teach a person anything. Making sense data significant meant that books should utilize pictures. Thinking of human nature as good and growth as natural meant that a school should be a garden in which children were growing.

Quintilian's faculty psychology led to the scientific problem of transfer of training. Locke and the doctrine of a blank tablet led to the association of ideas and from that to the scientific studies of the association of stimulus and response. Herbart and the doctrine of apperceptive mass led to the National Herbart Society, which changed its name twice, first to the National Society for the Scientific Study of Education and then to its present name, the National Society for the Study of Education, still publishing yearbooks dominantly conceived as science applied to practical problems of education. G. Stanley Hall has been called the first in a long line of scientific educational psychologists. The scientific child study that he founded, continues to prosper. Edward Lee Thorndike, a pupil of William James, created S-R bond psychology, or connectionism, and also created generations of educational scientists seeking laws of learning. J. M. Rice, in 1897, presented the first paper on the results of early measurement (spelling was the topic); and through A. Binet, Lewis Terman, and many others, the measurement school not only generated intelligence tests but extended statistical concepts and methods into a special study of its own. Characteristically, scientific studies of education have eschewed explicit normative views and have implicitly asserted the dominance of method over doctrine.

Little interchange occurs between the major modes of study: philosophy, common sense, and science. Uncritical coexistence rather than reflective cooperation among them marks the relation. Eclecticism is one consequence. One need only take a small pinch of philosophy here (for the "aims" chapter), bits of data and scientific findings scattered about here and there (for the "fact" of the matter), and an earnest commitment to have the common sense to apply everything aptly to any educational practice, and one has the so-called Foundations of Education. Muddle-making, not sense-making, is the upshot.

Sense-making structures, like educative events themselves, are ways human beings become more intelligent about themselves and their surroundings. We will need a device that helps us move without confusion back and forth, or up and down, between these two aspects of the problem. We will exploit the metaphor of the map and draw "concept maps" and "fact maps" and other sorts of maps so that we can locate ourselves as we move along. We will try to be careful to make clear the difference between what spectacle is being viewed (the educative events), and what spectacles, or conceptual goggles, we use to see with (the theory of educating).

We will move from the spectacle to the spectacles; each will contribute to the understanding of the other. To do so will require a theory of educating accounting for these difficulties and providing an explanation of educative events. An event epistemology relating events, facts and concepts to other elements of knowledge is a basic working heuristic named "The V." Through it we can establish artifactual regularities, invent concepts and theoretic structures, and move easily among levels of meaning generated out of educative events. An event epistemology will also help us to bring together the insights of conventional common sense, of various scientific claims, and the analytic and integrative power of contemporary philosophy. The starting point is always educative events, and each of four commonplaces of teacher, curriculum, learner, and social governance carries equal weight in these events; none is to be reduced to any other. The role of theory is to hold these concerns together so all can serve a proper role in improving our intelligence about educating.

The next chapter presents a theory of educating.

CHAPTER TWO

A Theory of Educating

For a beginning sense of direction, let us suppose that educating has to do with shaping human dispositions (beliefs, behaviors, actions) through the use of meaningful materials chosen according to criteria of excellence. Beliefs and behaviors of human beings can be shaped in a large variety of ways—indoctrination, conditioning, socialization, and so forth. These ways can be educative or miseducative. A street-corner sense of education is to "get smart." In everyday living there are hundreds of ways of getting smart, of developing savvy, of knowing what is coming down. Human beings do get smart from formal education as well, but this seems to be a well-kept secret. Formal education is not only a deliberate intervention in the lives of people, but an intervention with a highly selected and refined set of materials. These materials must be tailored for their meaningfulness and they must embody criteria of excellence. Furthermore, in formal education we believe that repeated events of deliberate intervention gradually shape habits such that *persons are liberated by and freed from both the intervention and the materials.* As durable and reliable as educational activities are, they are also short-lived and ephemeral; no single characterization will capture completely the whole scene. So, recognizing that we are not trying to define the ineffable, let us begin with a statement to serve as a working sense of direction.

> Educating, as an eventful process, changes the meaning of human experience by intervention in the lives of people with meaningful

materials, to develop thinking, feeling, and acting as habitual dispositions in order to make sense of human experience by using appropriate criteria of excellence.

Our sense of direction evolves around the notion of excellence. We are concerned with excellence because what is excellent must be conserved and must be progressively extended to all people in freedom. All free people will find their beliefs and behaviors shaped by grasping what is excellent. Excellence in a democratic society does not require elitism or any other artificial distinction of social class. Both major social traditions—the conservative and the progressive—require recognition of excellence and its role in changing, improving, and enlightening life experience. All major viewpoints of the social order also recognize that no society can continue to exist without one generation serving to educate the next. Education does not guarantee the survival of a preferred social order, of course. Education is neither a necessary nor a sufficient condition for human life. These observations make us realize the real strength of patterns of educating; we also see their complexities.

Our sense of direction, then, is to change the meaning of human experience. Our sense of approach is to intervene in the lives of human beings with materials that have passed appropriate tests. Clearly in human encounters we take the direction of liberating and not oppressing people in the process of educating.

Educating as an Eventful Process

It is usual to think of educating as a process, specifically a process of change, enduring through time to generate a product. In any study of education it is appropriate to distinguish between process and product. When the *object* of the educative process is a person, however, we usually hesitate to use the word "product" because of the unwanted analogies to mechanical process generating material products, like a factory making toy human beings. So we discuss events, process, change, time, and so forth in the context of persons.

The educative event is an intervention in the living of experience of persons, and this intervention is designed to change the meaning of experience for these human beings. The materials of instruction we use in educative intervention must pass certain tests, particularly tests of meaningfulness and educational excellence. How meaning develops from human experience and just what notion of meaning we use are legitimate questions.

Human experience and meaning should converge in educative events. Events are our focus of attention. Though events take place in time, it is difficult to measure the time it takes in terms of identifiable units. A minute is not a minute is not a minute. Educational time has no equal units. Realizing that it is extermely difficult to find the proper unit of time with which to describe educative episodes, I refrain from using clock hours or semester hours or Carnegie units or class periods or grade level or years of age. Using equal units of time as measures of educative episodes has been misleading, if not actually a major tyranny.

How long is Christmas? What unit of time measures emotional distress? a valid insight? mastery? We could draw from our experience with these human occurrences a sense of time. We could say that some insights came in a flash as an "ah-ha" experience, and other insights came very slowly. Mastery is usually slow, but it is much faster for some people than for others. Ridding ourselves of emotional distress is likewise more extended for some than others. These are nonchronological indices to the temporal quality of these matters. These indices are not composed of equal units of time. I am convinced of the episodic flow of educative events. That will have to suffice for the time.

Change is another concept required in a theory of education, and change is often related to some unit of time. Most concepts of education point to something that is changed as a consequence of educative events. This theory claims that the change is in the meaning of human experience. The two most popular education viewpoints, the behavioral and the classical, specify other changes education is supposed to make.

A behaviorist view held for a long time specifies that to educate is to change behavior, period. To educate is to cause behavior to change in line with prespecified objectives. To train a young person in the complex skills of safety and efficiency in driving a car, a long list of specific behaviors are identified, and the student practices until these behaviors become more or less automatic through a long process of overlearning. Children are taught table manners by various techniques like "token economies" based on concepts of behavior modification. Individuals learn to manipulate their own behavior to lose weight, to stop smoking, to exercise, by specifying in advance what the terminal behaviors are to be and then working to make behavior change so as to achieve these goals. Before J. B. Watson, before B. F. Skinner, before I. Pavlov, human beings used rewards (both given and withheld) to modify the behavior of horses, dogs, cats, slaves, children, adults. No doubt exists that behavior can be changed. Furthermore, by concentrating on observable changes in behavior, researchers in education have an objective basis for studying it. If the child can play the piano after instruction, the child's behavior has changed. If a student after instruction can work a mathematics problem, behavior has changed and education has done its job. We can and do change habits. But changing habits is only part of the process of educating.

These views are very popular in the United States. There is truth in them. Nevertheless, they override their validity and are extended into realms where they do not apply, and clever ad hoc verbal explanations do not save the theory. For example, it appears evident that we are doing something when we are thinking; we can stop, take thought, change our mind, get an idea. Yet none of these so-called behaviors is observable. The most common behavior found in schools, the listening of the pupils, is not directly observable. A person's feelings may be overtly expressed by a process of acting out—by crying, laughing, or fighting. But many feelings are known only as the person chooses to reveal them to others. How terrible it would be to have no privacy, no secrets of one's own immediate experience. It may be true that at the present time we overcontrol expressions of feeling, as I suspect we do, but since *feelings* and *thoughts* are behaviors and actions that are not necessarily observed at the time they occur, this serious limitation reflects adversely on the adequacy of behavior-change theories to account for educational change. Overt and observable changes in behavior do serve as *evidence*—for example, evidence for the inference that something educative has happened to the person. But to reduce educational episodes to behavior change is to be short-changed.

Classical views of education are also popular in the United States and in most other Westernized societies. These views too want the student to change, especially in respect to the sorts of products the student submits to the educational establishment for evaluation. They want better term papers, neater handwriting, better composition. They suppose that by getting these, they get better comprehension, greater knowledge, increased understanding. Evidence for these changes is found in the product submitted: examination books, papers, scores on schievement tests, class rank, prizes garnered. Such documents of achievement are taken to mean that an educative process has happened and that it is the cause of increase in information, knowledge, skill, understanding. One need not know how the process itself works as long as one has absolutely impeccable standards and absolutely reliable expert judges. External examiners can tell if the student has received an education very much as examining physicians can tell if a person has contracted a disease like the measles; the marks are evident.

Both these popular views take the *product* of the process as evidence of the process. Both assert that the process has some causal efficacy that benefits the product. And both assume that education has to do with fundamental changes in human beings. My theory is also a change theory, but it is much more concerned with studying what happens in the educative episodes at all places, not just the preset objectives and the terminal behaviors, or the products connoting achievement. I focus on changes in the meaning of experience of persons.

Changing the Meaning of Experience

To educate *is* to change the *meaning* of human experience. After a person has undergone an intentional educative event, the meaning of experience has changed for that person. The change in meaning will range from the trivial to the profound. The durability will also vary.

We understand the creation of meaning out of human experience when we understand that something (A) can come to stand for something else (B). The footprint in the sand is taken as a sign that a person probably walked there; the footprint that is present is a sign of the person who is absent. The footprint is a record of an event. If the ocean washes over the footprint, that record is destroyed; there is no remaining basis for a sign of those past events. We say that smoke is a sign of fire, and sometimes it is. We say that dark cloud are a sign of rain, and sometimes the rains do come. When we take something that is in present time (the footprint) to be a sign of something else, we are making inferences. We are also making meaning. When we say that "A is a sign of B" or that "A stands for B," we are also saying that "A means B." The footprint stands for or means a person. The smoke means that fire is likely; the clouds mean rain.

Social meaning is an achievement of shared human activity such that the *same sign* is taken to stand for the same event. Meaning is generated out of shared experience. While it is true that animals other than human beings have signal systems (elaborate in some cases), it does appear that only people develop languages with both sign and symbol systems. Symbols are signs that we respond to by developing a concept or by applying a concept. In thinking about meaning in our theory of educating, we shall focus primarily upon conceptual meanings, but let us not forget that sign meanings (as in body language) are also important vehicles for sharing meanings and thus undergoing the same experience. *This fact of sharing meanings so that we can undergo the same experience makes educating possible: meaning is social.* While it may appear from all that has been written so far that the social as a category has been left out, it is not so. The creation, refinement, and extension of meaning is social.

While meanings are constructed, our powers as human beings are roused; we come into their possession. But we also come into possession of our world. Meanings connect things. And it is this feature also that gives certain events their educational value. The construction of meanings connects the present to the past—the footprint to a person. They connect the present to the future—the clouds to the likelihood of rain. They connect events to causes both present and future. They also connect facts to principles and hope to memory. In these kinds of events, arising out of the construction of meanings, we discern our coming into possession not only of our powers but also of the world we live in. Educational value arises out of the construction of meanings that tie things together and thus create our world.

It seems evident that much human behavior is a quest for meaning. Some kind of meaning will be made out of any situation. A person searching for meaning will not rest until it has been established. Furthermore, meanings are extractable and transferable. A meaning created or developed in one situation may be extracted and implanted in another. This extraction and application to a different situation may be facilitated through teaching. To teach is to extend, change, or give new meanings to experience. Changing the meaning of experience does not necessarily result in immediate behavior change, but if meaning is changed and a student acts in the light of the changed meaning, behavior *may* be different. It is possible, however, for meanings to change and behavior to remain the same; in that event behavior can remain the same but its meaning as human action be different. Changing meaning and changing behavior are contingently, not causally, related in human experience. I distinguish behavior from action by saying that an action is a behavior with meaning.

The educational value of any object resides in its utility for assisting us to come into possession of our powers and come into possession of the world we inhabit. The possibility of educational worth, like the possibility of education itself, rests upon the fact that meanings are social constructions that, on the one hand allow us to exercise the powers of inference, self-understanding, and thoughtful action, and, on the other hand, tie things together in the world we inhabit.

Grasping the meaning, especially of materials that embody the criteria of excellence, is fundamental to the educative process. The notion of grasped meaning is ordinarily expressed in statements such as : "He has a sense of it"; "She got it, by golly, she got it"; "He has the hang of it"; "Now I see what you mean"; "So that's the point, eh"; "If you just see this, all the rest follows"; "You mean Caliban, Ariel, and Prospero stand for the tripartite soul of the Renaissance Man!" It is the act that each of us must do for ourselves, even though we require extensive help from others. Learning, really *learning,* the materials to the point of mastery, is the responsibility of the individual that cannot be shared. Learning takes place after one has already grasped the meaning: *it is the grasped meaning that one learns.* Grasping meaning is not the same thing as learning. Take the example of catching on to a joke: do we learn all the jokes that make us laugh? The satisfying discharge that comes from genuine laughter makes us feel better and in some ways think more clearly. But unless we undertake some active effort to remember the joke, we will not automatically learn it by just getting the point of it. Of course, some people are such swift learners that they do quickly go from grasping meaning to assimilating the grasped meaning into their cognitive structure. But these are separable events, meaning and learning. (See below, Chapter 5, for further discussion.)

The notion of meaning is a major plank in the theory of educating. To teach is to try deliberately to change the meaning of students' experience, and students must grasp the meaning before they deliberately learn something new. Learning is never entirely cognitive. Feelings accompany any thinking that moves to reorganize meaning. In educating we are concerned to integrate thinking, feeling, and acting. Return to the example of humor. In order to learn to tell a joke, we must first "get the point" of the joke. The example is fruitful. Consider the dismay that is felt when after telling a joke, someone says, "I don't get it!" To explain the joke by making the argument of the joke explicit always destroys the joke. We must get the point, but we cannot be given the point. Getting the point is the first and necessary step; then we can learn to tell the joke. (Note that "getting it" in the case of jokes always requires making an inference, even in the case of sight jokes.) In such cases, and indeed probably in all cases, what we learn first is the point, the grasped meaning. What follows is the possibility of new learning, learning to *tell* the joke.

In grasping the meaning of a joke, we are also doing something else: we *feel* something. Jokes and other forms of humor which make us laugh are occasions when feelings are expressed. Often in the context of educating, a teacher may make a point and find the student response is laughter. Sometimes in philosophy classes when a student catches on to the point of an argument, spontaneous laughter occurs. Skilled lecturers can tell if their audience is with them if laughter accompanies a significant point. Nor is laughter the only index of the connection between feelings and grasped meaning: anger, fear, shame, affection, liking, and desiring are other indices of feelings that accompany thinking.

A powerful moment in educating occurs when grasping the meaning and feeling the significance come together. When human feelings merge into meaning, we achieve a way to make sense of experience. I call this connection between feelings and meaningfulness "felt significance"—a name for the conception of value which I think is fundamental to educating.

A Conception of Value

The sun warms; we feel it immediately; spontaneously and naively we respond to it. We do not necessarily think about it at the time we enjoy the feeling directly, but once we begin to think about the simple goodness of warn sun, we have already moved to a meaning that is mediated by concepts of warmth, self, joy. As soon as we begin to develop a sense of desiring to repeat the feeling (or to keep the feeling in existence), we are already on our way to a process of valuing: the value event, the sun warming us, has happened. Our memory is a record of the event; thinking and acting come into play in the service of making the good feeling last; feelings are connected with ideas of their significance. Value is felt significance. The construct of both feelings and significance is necessary because we can have one without the other. We have feelings without meaning: "I like art, but I don't know what it means," and we can have meaning without feeling: "I know art, but I don't know what I like."

Most of the time, human beings respond not to raw events but to the meaning of events. We judge events for their import, for what is likely to follow from them. Import suggests importance, a test of further connections in experience. Some of these meanings undoubtedly refer to such qualities as enjoyment, suffering, liking, prizing, shunning, fearing, hating, loving. As we sort through these various ordinary human experiences, we generally determine what they mean for us by relating them to their source, their direct experience, and to their upshot—that is, to antecedents, consummations, and their consequences. Out of the ground of meanings such as these, value as felt significance emerges.

Felt significance is a magnifying glass of focusing meanings, making them intense to the point of recognizable significance. As we grasp meanings, we may feel significance. The feeling of the significance—the connection-making—is the basis of value in experience. When we are listening to a teacher or reading a book or writing or paying attention to a conversation, we are grasping meanings. When we also feel the significance, we are making another connection: we are adding value. Meaning is both a prior condition and an ingredient in events that have value.

Another example concerns the way the sciences of chemistry and biology use the word "valence." The root meaning is that of *valere,* to be strong, but the scientific usage moves away from the root. The common usage in biology and chemistry for valence is indicating a power "to combine with." Thus a technical definition of valence in chemistry is the capacity of an element or radical to combine with another, as measured by the number of hydrogen atoms which one radical or one atom of the element will combine with or replace. Oxygen, then, has a value, or valence, of two, which means that one atom of oxygen combines with two hydrogen atoms. It has been said that amino acids are the basis of organic life, and of amino acids it is the *affinity* of one carbon atom for another carbon atom that permits amino-acid chains. In genetics, from Mendel on, the genetic theory has sought to explain the separation (segregation, Mendel called it), and recombination of pieces of genetic matter. Both the chemical basis of life and the genetic basis of continuity of life seem to require a coming together and a separating. The *selective affinity* of one thing for another, the capacity of one thing to combine with another, is a remarkable feature which is the basis of value in nature.

One more example from human experience. Erich Fromm, in *The Art of Loving.* declares that "love is the answer to the problem of human existence." This problem, stated simply, is separation. Human beings, instructed in a language, become aware of the self as an object. We come to understand that each of us is alone. The telling question for human beings is "how to overcome separateness, how to achieve union, how to transcend one's own individual life and find at-onement" (Fromm, 1970). Fromm claims that interpersonal fusion found in productive love is the best solution. Work also helps. In creative work the person unites the self with materials which represent the world outside the self; worker and object become united. Creative and productive work requires me to plan, and actively to produce a result for which I can be responsible. In love and work a fusion overcomes separation. Individuality is also preserved because the fusion is a *relation* between separated parts, not an obliteration of one by the other. The deceptively simple formula for what it means for an adult to reach maturity was given by Freud: to be able to love and to work. Fromm and Freud appear to agree about this fundamental view.

Examples such as these and others like them have brought me to some convictions about value. I view value in natural events and objects, and in social events that people share as that quality which combines things otherwise separate and connects people otherwise alone and alientated. *Value is what holds things together.* And judgments of value (value claims) constructed through science and other rational ways tell us which combinations are significant, which things fit together, and why.

Are there things which combine, and persons who establish relations, which are not good? Can "combining power" and "connection making" be bad? My defense is similar to Dewey's defense of the concept of growth. (Dewey 1916) Growth is good if it contributes to more growth; growth is bad if it leads to dead ends, truncated experience, severe limitations on the possibilities of further growth. So, in my case, connections are good if they lead to further connections, to enrichments, to the artistic intensification of experience which we sometimes see in "peak experiences" (Maslow's notion), those times in our lives when everything is going our way. Most adults who have known productive love, work, and education can refer to such actual experiences. The fact is, good things come and go, things are good while they last as good, and then something else moves in to take their place. We experience loss.

Each loss is also a chance for a new start, each experience of pain is also a chance to think rationally about alternatives and to plan differently. Each break-up and separation unwanted by the participants is a chance to review the grounds and conditions for other and maybe better relations. Just as feelings surge and subside and intensify experience, so too do good things pulse and pass. The wonder is that they sometimes return.

Educating is significant when it generates connections in experience, when it overcomes separation and creates human harmony. What are we connecting? For the individual person we are bringing together thinking and feeling and acting. For persons in a social setting we are bringing together purposes that can be shared, a sense of mutuality and mutual accommodation. Love and work are productive values for human beings. I would add education, for the acts of educating and their products endow us with the ability to connect things, to separate things, and to see why such connections are significant.

We come into the world through birth, but we come into possession of our powers only through education. Education is that process by which we come into possession of our powers for the exercise of intellect, emotion, imagination, judgment, and action. It is also a process by which we come to self-understanding, including the capacity to change our minds. If any object, program, pattern of instruction, and so forth has educational value, this value resides in its utility for education, for helping us to come into possession of our powers. Hence, to say that one educational program or object is educationally better than another is to say that it has more educational value. It contributes more to our coming into possession of our powers as human beings.

When we help a student make a meaningful connection between his or her personal constructs and the conceptual structures of academic disciplines, we must add "significance" if such educating is to have value. The student must experience the *significant* connection through feelings to achieve felt significance. Thinking is not enough, nor is mindless acting. Nor am I recommending the total indulgence in feelings shorn of thinking and acting. Rather, the flourishing integration of thinking and feeling and acting is a mark of an educated person.

The educative process generates "human capital," it adds

value, it creates value. In the marketplace of ideas very little cost is incurred in comparison to the benefits accrued. When a teacher gives an idea to a student and the student in response gives another idea to the teacher, both have gained an idea but neither has lost one. When your values generate values, as love creates love, as educating begets the educated and they become educators, value-making has a multiplier-effect (as in Keynesian economics). Significance is the value name for the increase in meaningful connections in experience.

What Makes the Eventful Process Happen?

A brief answer can be given: the educative process takes place as people come together over a curriculum in their social roles of teachers, learners, governors. It is the *interaction* of the four commonplaces that makes the eventful process happen. We have a shifting back-and-forthness between teachers and students as they bring their diverse knowledge and experience to bear upon the new material of the curriculum. There is a testing, and a testing out, of new as well as old meanings. There is a shifting up and down between levels of meanings; between the concrete and the abstract, between the conceptual and the factual, between the imaginary and the actual, between the claims on our attention which turn out to be false and those which pass some test of truthfulness, and so forth.

For experience to show a gain in educative significance, two basic changes must occur for the *person as a learner.* There must be an increase in both effective intelligence and emotional responsiveness. The educative process uses meaningful materials to develop persons' intelligence as an habitual disposition. This habit is aimed at the search, analysis, and articulation of meaning in human experience by using criteria of excellence appropriate to a comprehensive range of human experience. Within this comprehensive range there are many forms of excellence, and diverse criteria of what makes something count as excellent. These diverse forms, criteria and making of excellence, are typically associated with different large domains of human effort: the sciences, the arts, mathematics, philosophy, history, politics, craftsmanship, practical skills. Deliberate instruction can be given to help persons *recover meaning* from canned or fixed bodies of knowledge and other codified records of human experience. Such studies of the structure of knowledge identify criteria of excellence (see below, Chapter 4). And deliberate help can be given, up to apoint, to help persons use such reconstructed meanings to *reorganize meaning* of their own personal experience (below, Chapter 5). Intelligence-in-use is the active, persistent, and careful consideration of any claims, beliefs, or belief system in the light of the grounds that support them and the further inferences and interpretations to which they might be connected.

A proximate function of the educative process is to foster the union of benevolent impulse and intelligent reflection. Dewey thought that in this union the role of thoughtful inquiry was as important as that of sympathetic affection. A person can become intelligent about emotional responsiveness. It is important not to deny the existential reality of *feelings.* A person feels angry, or fearful, or zestful. These direct feelings are events. As events they just happen. And there is nothing good or bad, true or false, right or wrong about these events. As events they are necessary conditions for the creation of concepts of value and the establishment of factual judgments about direct experience. To develop persons with open channels and free interplay between direct feelings and directed intelligence is highly likely to result in human action that is good for human beings. We have more to say about feelings in Chapter 5.

Learners and Learning

Learning in the context of educating is a process under the deliberate control of the learner. The learner is the efficient cause of learning. Learning is something the person does for him or her self, it is individual and idiosyncratic. Learning, and learning about learning, thus *should* be part of the self-interest of the person. It *should* be so, but individuals are not always aware of what their own best self-interests are. Educating can help people comprehend what is at stake for them in educative events.

A person's self-interest in educative events might well be described as the deliberate connection-making between thinking and feeling which leads to intentional human acting. Thinking and feeling and acting are intensely personal matters. Often these personal matters become separated from one another, and their relations are not seen or understood. Too much of ordinary schooling is limited to thinking; feeling and acting are somehow to take care of themselves. But the best sense of educating should sustain a flourishing integration of thinking, feeling, and acting. This integration is the person's self-interest.

Why? These three elements need each other. Thinking needs feeling in order to operate; thought by itself moves nothing; feeling shorn of thinking is without direction. Acting in an intentional way validates both thinking and feeling. Acting tests ideas; it arouses and expresses feeling. Thinking leads to acting because thinking helps us to see and comprehend alternatives. Thinking shows us that things could be otherwise; thinking supplies us with a way to get beyond the evils of the moment; thinking establishes a basis in the regularities of knowledge and value claims so things can truly become closer to what is desirable. Acting with an interest based on thinking and feeling is a powerful individual mode of learning. Changing the meaning of human experience through educating comes from integrating thinking, feeling, and acting. Learners who understand this point of educating can become self-interested and self-directed learners.

Most standard education theories make the nature of human nature central. This theory does not, but acknowledges the importance of persons in calling for the kind of person who can become intelligent about becoming intelligent, who can learn about learning. The person is also recognized as significant in that it is a person who chooses, a person who makes meaning out of experience, a person who creates the knowledge and values embedded in educative materials. *It takes a person who has understood something to recognize when another person has also understood.*

It seems clear that *inventiveness* is a characteristic of those who make sense of their experience. What is appropriately changing cannot be finally specified. Other than seeing that we want an educated person to be the product of the educative process (which is not the appalling tautology some think it to be, since some educative processes defeat themselves), the nature of the person cannot be reduced to an "essence." We recognize persons who find, test, and extend meanings in their experience. They are in all walks of life. They might be philosopher-kings, or the democratically socialized individual, or the cultured esthete. They could be the artisan, the warrior, the courtier, the feminist, the athlete, or some combination of parts of all of these. It seems futile to denote with precision what specific kind of person education should aim to develop. We can enjoin others to celebrate the diversity and uniqueness of persons, to prize rather than to despise differences, and to find openness and creativity as well as discipline and precision to be of value. In denying some sort of essence in personhood, we are just asserting that we cannot specify in advance what specific personal outcomes the educative process must generate. How varied and complex are the products of the educative process!

Who would not want to live a life of zest and intelligent responsiveness to the world and to other persons? A rational, cooperative, caring, loving life is possible for every one. As Fromm notes, (1970) the art of loving is based on knowledge as much as on feeling. And knowledge is based on the freedom that comes with the power to generate new meanings for oneself and for others; new meanings about personhood, new meanings about ideas that make sense, new meanings about experience and nature. The creation of new meanings for oneself and for others comes from intelligently considered educative events. As events, they are eventful: Something matters, something follows, something is *consequential.* It is meaning that makes biological creatures alive in the fullest sense. It is meaning, of course, that makes social creatures social, and permits the liberation of individuals from the oppressive coercion of social structures. Sexual freedom or freedom from racial tyrannies or relief from social class humiliations or freedom from demeaning labor are at base freedoms created by intelligence. Education puts intelligence to work in its most powerful forms in its most diverse and richly varied contexts. We can choose. It is our choice if we make it our choice. The most powerful freedom is the freedom of thought, for that can be controlled by no external agency once we have won the grounds for creating meaning out of human experience and nature. Once you truly think for yourself, you have a freedom that, as Dewey wrote, "No external defeats can nullify."

Choice is central, too, in this concept of educating. Making choices, like making inferences, is the daily business of most human beings. It is so omnipresent that we fail to recognize it. Being aware of our choices is difficult. Among the most subtle, elusive, and significant of our frequent choices are the times we *choose to pay attention* (James 1950:402, "My experience is what I agree to attend to"). Imagine yourself in a classroom, a lecture, a sermon, a film, a political speech, an advertising commercial. Your attention shifts from on to off at a whim. What catches your attention? What is it out of all that flows across your scanning devices that deserves your focus? What is it that you notice? Basically, unless a person is physically ill, drugged, brainwashed, or otherwise not in control of normally functioning sensing devices, a person *chooses* to pay attention or not. As a teacher or friend or salesman or preacher or politician, we can badger, cajole, persuade, or otherwise try to gain the attention of our listeners. But if they choose not to listen, choose to turn off our broadcasting messages, those messages do not get through. Extending an educative meaning is something like giving another a loaf of bread with love. It is not forced feeding.

Think about the fragility of giving a thing to another person (Peirce 1958). If a teacher puts something forth, does the student have to take it? Suppose you try to give a pencil to a student. To take it from you the student has to pay attention, to focus on the pencil and not your hand. The intention to take the object may be the slightest one can imagine, but some intention must be there; that is, some choice to receive what you give has to be made. To think twice about taking something given is to recognize the power of choice, to take or not to take it.

If the teacher puts something forth—an idea, a diagram, a proposition, a puzzle—the student who has chosen to pay attention responds not merely to the chalk marks or the noise patterns but to these movements as a sign of an index of something else. The student's attention is transferred from the teacher's direct movements to the object (the idea, thing, new event) to which the teacher points. Instead of regarding the object as a stimulus, the student responds in a way that is a function of the teacher's relationship, actual and potential, to the object. The student responds to the object put forth as having meaning that can be grasped. Taking the meaning of what has been put forth as meaningful by the teacher is the student's task. The meaning of the object, idea, or new event has supplied the basis for the interaction of student and teacher.

Taking the meaning, grasping it, provides the bridge to possible learning. We can learn meanings we have grasped. Also, the student deliberately and voluntarily chooses to try to fit the newly grasped meaning into what the student already knows. The student is learning. Grasping meanings is a frequent experience only sometimes attended by acts of learning. When learning begins to take on a life of its own, other choices become recognizable. Not only can one begin to choose which topics to study, which interest to follow, which specific talents to develop, but one can also choose to learn about learning. And after this point is reached, one can consciously choose to be educated, and then one can choose to become self-educating. When this point is reached, the person is largely free from formal intervention; the person has the power, the positive freedom, for further learning. The power of choice, coupled with effective action, creates that wonderful feeling of driving with one's head above the traffic, seeing what is favoring and what is problematic, comprehending a lot from a little, having a strong sense of taking charge of one's life. Choice is heady stuff.

Choice, of course, is never entirely free. If we are faced with two white pills that look alike, we are not entirely free to choose which one we want to be aspirin and which one arsenic. There is something in the matter which matters. Objects, it has been said from sad experience, are things which object. Natural events happen without our choice. In educating, the teacher has power of choice initially about which of all the available materials are to be analyzed and reconstructed into educative materials. Even the teacher, however, is not free to decide that *The Tempest* is purple rock salt. The educative materials we use are materially significant to freely chosen human actions partly because they are the things they are.

Teachers and Teaching

Teachers are the efficient cause of teaching. Teachers are therefore responsible for teaching. For teachers to assume this responsibility properly, the office of the teacher (the place of the teacher in the institution of education) is given certain powers. Expectations about teachers roles are fairly fixed, even standardized to a point of stereotyping. Teachers are perceived to be an authority, with commensurate rights, and to be, upon occasion, authoritarian, without commensurate duties restricting oppressive authoritarianism. We think positively of teaching as an intentional process of trying to get some other person to do something, or to think about something that that person cannot now do. Teaching changes the other person by intervention in his life with certain materials selected to make sense of human experience. We think negatively about intervention. It seems to cause us problems because it can be heavy-handed, too powerful, too easily a slippage from authority to authoritarianism.

The word "intervention" has a negative cast. In political terms it is an action of one state forcing another to change in order to protect the interests of the first state. Intervention between quarreling parties also suggests interference to affect the interests of others. What of educational intervention? In educating we are initiating an action, not waiting benignly for something good to happen so we can reward it. We are making definite claims on others. We recognize prior existence of relevant claims, however, and educational intervention is a coming between self-interest and subject-interest, an interruption of ongoing experience. Continuing in a state of innocent nature will not establish education. We soften the blow somewhat by carefully defining the circumstances and conditions of proper intervention, but we must intervene.

How do we soften the blow? What does it mean to come between self-interest and subject interest? First it is a responsibility of both teacher and student to be concerned with the student's self-interest. Students are often unaware of their own best interest, and teachers should know they have a responsibility to help students become aware of what the student already knows, and especially those prepotent ways by which the student makes sense of experience and nature. The new meanings will be learned in terms of the old meanings, including misconceptions as well as proper conceptions in the pattern of old meanings. Second, the teacher has a responsibility to become consciously aware of the teacher's authority in interpreting the subject to the student. The teacher must see clearly the relation between the XYZ meanings of the discipline and the ABC meanings the teachers take responsibility for,—namely, the teacher's authority. I use the shorthand "XYZ materials" to stand for all bodies of knowledge; and "ABC materials" to stand for retrieved meanings from these bodies of knowledge that have been reconstructed for teaching purposes. Third, both student and teacher come together to establish congruence of meaning. The teacher teaches the ABC meanings to students; students grasp the meaning of these ABC meanings; the teacher-student interaction is a testing for congruence—namely, that the meanings of the ABC materials which the teacher intends the student to grasp are in fact the meanings the students take away from the interaction. The fourth step is the students': to work, study, rehearse, practice, act, etc., to understand how the meaning of experience has been or could be changed as a consequence of incorporating the new meanings into the old meaning structure with which the student is working. The actual learning is caused by the action of the learner, not the teacher. The various products the student makes—for example, written papers, performances, expressions of interest—can be taken by the teacher as evidence that the student's previously organized pattern of meaning is now reorganized into a new pattern. Fifthly, the student becomes aware of access to the XYZ materials independently of the teacher's ABC interpretation. The student, no longer dependent upon the teacher, uses the criteria of excellence of the materials as a way to make sense of nature and human experience.

Curriculum

It should be obvious that the freely chosen human actions are central to this theory of educating. Not so obvious, perhaps, is the centrality of *educative materials.* These meaningful materials are significant in several ways. First of all, they carry with them appropriate criteria of excellence. For some materials the central excellence is a version of knowledge and truth. For others, criteria of beauty, elegance, and artistic merit dominate. Still other materials exhibit criteria of human judgment, like justice in politics, fairness in ethics, meaningfulness in education. Since these criteria are to be found in the XYZ materials and retrieved for use in educating, they are criteria that are public, open, definite. These public, open qualities help enormously in reducing oppression in educative episodes. The teacher does not unilaterally control the access to the XYZ materials; the student can learn to be free of any teacher once a legitimate way into the XYZ materials has been found and tested, and as it makes sense of the students' experience. As will be discussed below in Chapter 6, there exists a fundamental relation between freedom and authority, a relation that gives legitimate power to human experience.

A second value in educative materials is the increase in intelligence which they permit. We do not, each one of us, have to begin in the blindest ignorance of what's around and what's significant to us. We can learn from what others produce, and this learning can be a very efficient, inexpensive process. When a proof is formulated in mathematics, a work of art is produced in literature, a code of justice is established in law, there is little additional cost whether the meaning of these products are understood by one person or a thousand. When a teacher puts forth an idea to a class of students, the teacher does not give it away in the sense of not having it anymore. All the students who grasp the idea "get it" and the teacher still "has it." Thus meaning multiplies in an educative episode. We all can stand on the shoulders of giants.

Educative materials can be seen as *records of prior events* which *human beings can use to make new events happen.* A third value in educative materials is the way they guide events. To some extent these materials are like maps, code books, architectural drawings, written musical scores. They are guides to events. If you understand the map, you may take a trip; if you understand the code, you could send and receive messages; if you understand drawings, you might build a house; if you read musical scores, you may be able to make beautiful music with others.

For materials to qualify as educative materials, they must be analyzed (logically and pedagogically) for their meaning structure so some meanings can be extracted. These recovered meanings must be reconstructed into forms that permit sharing in the student-teacher interaction. The recovery from XYZ and the reconstruction into ABC materials is a curricular task, some of which is completed before teaching is initiated and some of which is generated through teacher-student planning during the educative episodes. After the educative episodes have been completed, teachers are free, of course, to continue work on their curricular tasks in preparation for subsequent educative acts.

Governance

We all know that the activities of educating take place in a social setting. Sharing experience, sharing meaning, and sharing purposes all necessarily require a social setting. But this basic fact does not tell us how the social setting can be a governing influence on the educative process. The fourth commonplace is, then, a general concern with the social mileux and a particular concern with social control. The general concern will find expression through concepts of ethics and social philosophy; the particular concern will find expression through concepts of administration. Let us begin with an example of administration.

Recently an elementary school principal told the teachers the school policy on reading. He complained that research on reading was so complex and so conflicting in points of view that a proper decision about the reading program was difficult to find. Therefore, he decided this school would use the SRA-Distar program throughout the grades. This is an example of how an act of governance *controls the meaning that controls the effort.* Most devices of social control work this way: controlling meaning which controls effort. Classroom management, as teachers well know, requires social control, too. The teacher can act just as the school principal did in deciding what things are to mean for the pupils. For example, a teacher might say: "We'll read the first two chapters before the field trip so you will have some idea what we are to see there." And a pupil might respond, "Is it okay if I just outline these chapters?" The pupil is deciding what meaning will control his effort. So, administration is not limited to administrators. Teachers act as governors; even pupils find ways to exercise a modicum of social control.

How can we think about social control? Concept from ethics

(for example, the relation between rights and duties) and from social philosophy are most relevant to issues of social control. The key concept is social justice. The key principle of social justice calls upon us to judge the claims of each person in the context of all persons. In a sense governance is a balancing act; it respects claims of teachers, pupils, administrators, parents and others in the community insofar as they have a relevant bearing upon the acts of educating. The curriculum in a very special way also presents claims we must pay attention to in educating. When claims come into conflict (e.g., through a scarcity of actual resources the teacher may not have enough time for all pupils), a decision about what is fair must be made. We can try to treat equals equally becuase we believe the same treatment for them is fair. And we can try to treat unequals unequally because we believe that compensatory treatment required by relevant differences is also fair. The principles of social justice give us the intellectual framework we need for the practical problems of governance.

Some social control is benign, some harsh. We need concepts and principles of governance which will exert effective control over educating. Abstractly stated, proper governance of educative events actualizes intended connections between teachers, curriculum, and learners so that events come to closure so that perceptible change in the meaning of experience has taken place. Unfortunately, controlling the meaning of educative events can be both liberating and oppressive.

Oppressive education is demeaning. Like racism and sexism, oppressive schoolism occurs unwittingly. It is a well-disguised force in the social structure. Often in the name of education we miseducate. It is important that we recognize a fundamental watershed between the educating process that is liberating and all the others that are oppressive.

Let us give the devil his due. On any account of frequency or popularity the compulsory, unchosen educative events take place most often. Behaviors are shaped and belief systems are implanted without the person really making educational choices. Quite often children who are the victims of these external forces are made to appear to be the cause of their own misery. They are told they come into the world as wounded and sinful creatures and it is appropriate that they get the devil beaten out of them. They are blamed for being immature even though any learner is immature in the beginning. They are put down for being uppity, made to feel dumb for being "too smart." To call a person ignorant insults rather than congratulates that person for having the power to come to know, to get smart, to become intelligent about nature and experience.

The process of internalized oppression works its harmful way into the school lives of both good and poor students. Poor students are those for whom the miseducative process creates expectations of "dumbness" or "stupidity." These students begin to believe they have "learning difficulties," that they are not very smart, that they can always expect to be in the lower ranks of students. Coming to expect less of themselves, they actually achieve less, and the records of events are taken as evidence of their inadequacies. Distress sets in and occludes chances for further educative change. The plight of "poor" learners is well known in schools.

The plight of the best students is less well known. Some of the "best" are victimized by the same process of internalized oppression. How does this process work? In typical schooling situations a small percentage of students are given top grades. They are the acknowledged leaders. They come to believe they are good students. They get the A's, and teachers reward them by accepting them into the protective inner circle of esteem and affection. Such validation is purchased with fear of failure. Successful students, when unaware of criteria of excellence as independent grounds for their success, come to fear failure. Moreover, they come to believe that being "right" or "correct" is the price for being loved and accepted. They learn to take few intellectual risks. They seldom disagree with teachers. They learn to control their behavior with a "win, do not lose" attitude. And they learn to suppress their feelings, especially negative feelings.

This schooling process works to disenfranchise both good and bad students. Students learn not to trust their own experience; they do not expect schooling to help make sense of things for them; they box in the events of schooling and, if they are lucky, begin to develop other ways to test reality so they can grow and mature.

Should we blame the students? Their teachers? Analysis of the oppression reveals that the oppressors were themselves oppressed. Those who grew up with tyranny are better prepared to use its techniques than they are prepared to find new and better ways of acting. Teachers once were students, just as parents once were children. Some beginning teachers make noises like experienced teachers; new parents find themselves saying and doing things their parents did to them under similar circumstances. In the most extreme cases, battered children are abused by adults who themselves were battered children. It is bootless to attribute blame, for both teachers and parents are doing the best they can; but the oppressors must come to understand their own history of oppression before the vicious cycle can be broken. They must experience alternative ways of controlling and validating their own experience before they can properly organize educative episodes that change the meaning of experience. Controlling the meaning of experience is a process that can be both liberating and oppressive.

Controlling the *meaning* of what is valid information is a powerful control over others. Concepts found in adult life to control others are (1) concepts created to evaluate others and (2) concepts that attribute motivations to others ("mind-reading"). The basic act of creating a concept whose meaning is given by us to others and whose validity is defined by us for others makes them feel controlled. Teachers perform these acts in the line of duty. They give grades or gold stars to pupils, and in judging the pupil's worth they keep the pupil in place. Pupils are told: "You want to be quiet and line up for lunch, now don't you?" "You want to study algebra so you'll be a proud engineer some day, don't you?" The teachers never wait for a reply. The teachers must control the class. The means of governance in the social psychology of the classroom have to do with controlling concepts that carry meaning, using concepts to evaluate (that is, to establish the criteria of what counts as success), and using concepts to tell what makes sense of a person's own experience. To be governed by these external forces is to be oppressed. As Plato said, to be a slave is to accept your purposes in life as given to you by others. To be free from oppressive forces is to understand the controls of meaning and to create independent gounds for deriving meaning from experience. Educating that changes the meaning of experience for the person works to free the individual from the act of intervention and from the specific curriculum used in educating. When teachers and learners are explicitly aware of the complex ways educating works, they can more freely participate in the process. Not only are we participants *in* educating, we also have knowledge *of* educating. We must understand the interactions of the four commonplaces in order to make educative events happen. This understanding helps us *in* the practice because it is a theory *of* that practice.

Let us consider a review of the theory of educating as I have developed it so far.

In the Preface and in Chapters 1 and 2 this theory is constructed to pay attention to distinctive events of educating. We see the commonplaces of teacher, curriculum, learning, and governance as necessary and as necessarily interacting with one another. In the course of analyzing these matters, I have introduced a number of new concepts: event, excellence, claim, grasped meaning, felt significance, the V. They have been combined conceptually in a way that I believe makes sense.

Sense-making structures, like educative events, are ways human beings become more intelligent about themselves and their surroundings. A good theory is one of the best sense-making structures we can devise. But it must be a theory that fits itself to the events of interest. My stress on the word "educating" is calculated to call attention to the *event sense* of the process of education.

Why events? If educating is an activity, we must be concerned with events. We make events happen when we govern so as to bring teaching and learning together with the curriculum. Furthermore, when we focus on an event as our unit of analysis, we see our way clear to both facts and concepts. Facts as records of events, and concepts as signifying regularities in events, are generated *out* of events. Our educating requires us to bring together the four commonplaces in an educative event.

Educating, then, is an activity and a set of activities. Events are made to happen as well as simply occurring haphazardly. When we make events of educating happen deliberately, we need to see that our modes of *thinking* about these prepotent events are of the utmost importance. Thinking and theorizing in a rational, systematic, and comprehensive manner should be our first concern. Taking thought in order to take action is a responsible thing to do, and when we are working with human beings, we must constantly be alert to our responsibilities, the rights of others, and the reasons justifying actions. Constructing a good theory, then, is a way out of our difficulties.

CHAPTER THREE

Teaching

Teaching is central to educating. We cannot have educating without teaching. The notion of teaching is the first one of the four commonplaces I have selected for analysis and definition. The analysis is of the activity of teaching and the definition is of a conception of teaching. In thinking of teaching as an activity, I am not setting out to describe roles and functions of teachers in schools; rather, I am concerned to think of teaching in the process of educating, wherever that occurs. Teachers are the efficient cause of teaching, and although the point of teaching concerns learning through shared meaning, teaching is not the cause of learning. Teaching, in the context of educating, is a social event in which human beings come to share meaning. Sharing meaning between persons is a large part of the process of changing the meaning of human experience.

An Analysis of Concepts

Teaching is the achievement of shared meaning in the context of educating. This conception of teaching requires some elucidation. Using educative materials of the curriculum, teacher and student aim at congruence of meaning. It is as if teacher and student were standing side by side looking together at the curriculum. (The teacher is not the curriculum; the teacher is not trying to teach himself.) In a teaching moment, the teacher acts intentionally to change the meaning of the student's experience, using curriculum materials. In a moment of choosing to pay attention to the teacher and the materials, the student acts intentionally to grasp meaning. The aim is shared meaning. A back-and-forthness between teacher and student can be brief or can last a long time, but the aim is to achieve shared meaning. In this interaction both teacher and student have definite responsibilities. The teacher is responsible for seeing to it that the meanings of the materials the student grasps are the meanings the teacher intended for the student to take away. The student is responsible for seeing to it that the grasped meanings are the ones the teacher intended. When these separate responsibilities are fulfilled and shared meaning is achieved, an episode of teaching has happened.

This "mutual unconcealment" in teaching requires reciprocity of responsibilities. We need to recognize that teaching cannot achieve shared meaning if the student does not participate. Just as a person has a right if and only if another has a duty to honor that right, teaching requires "studenting." Perhaps we have not paid enough attention to this role of students in the educative process. The term "studenting" is inelegant, to say the least; we need new terminology—for example, "responsive listener," "meaning sharer,"—to focus on this special role of students.

After teaching has resulted in shared meaning, the student is ready to decide whether to learn or not. Choosing to learn a grasped meaning is a responsibility of the learner that cannot be shared. Each of us is responsible for our own learning. This responsibility, and the attendant choices, are points of potential liberation. Usually it is not without determined effort that we learn as we reorganize the meanings of our lives. Such determinations are conditioned by choices. As we intelligently pursue our responsibilities for learning, we grow in power of choice, in power of action, and in flexibility of thinking. These responsibilities are surely worth caring for.

Teaching demands a special responsibility, too. Teaching requires authority. One of the greatest disasters to befall educational practice has been the miscomprehension of subject-matter knowledge. Teachers-to-be were supposed to get their knowledge from subject-matter disciplines, and some did. But knowledge given out in the form of "bodies of knowledge" is not the highly selected knowledge needed for teaching. The specialized knowledge and value claims of disciplines must be reworked for use in teaching. The teacher's authority is based on the reformulation of the XYZ materials pedagogy requires. Teachers-to-be need to understand and use the epistemology of their field as the basis for reconstructing claims. This special responsibility for selecting, analyzing, and reshaping primary claims for purposes of educating is the interaction between teaching and curriculum (see below, Chapter 4).

Other Views: The Behavioral and Classical

Let me now present two other major concepts of teaching—the behavioral and the classical—in order to define the boundaries of the one I prefer. One view, the behaviorists, slides from teaching into considering learning as change in behavior. The other view, the classicists, retreats from teaching back into the materials of instruction as knowledge to be mastered. Let us see briefly how the familiar fallacy of Changing the Topic occurs.

Strange as it may seem to some psychologists, both B. F. Skinner and Carl Rogers are here in the same camp. Skinner, Rogers, and their followers are all neutral with respect to knowledge. It does not matter to them whether physics or phrenology is to be taught; astrology or astronomy would do just as well. Mathematics or magic can change a person's behavior, and a Rogerian teacher can facilitate the learning of anything. In teaching, Rogerians reduce knowledge to what helps facilitate comfort and openness in the learner. Skinnerians reduce teaching to changes in behavior. *Both confuse teaching with learning.*

Classical views of teaching make subject-matter knowledge central. So central is it, in fact, that the student is almost totally forgotten. It is easy to see how two competing views keep each other alive: oscillation between a person-centered and a knowledge-centered view is necessary because each leaves out something necessary. The knowledge-centered classical views of teaching make a great to-do about explicating texts. The *text* is the key. From comprehensive reading lists (a whole library would be ideal) to well-wrought instructional packages to programmed instruction to computer-assisted instruction, the main element in teaching is a *thing,* is *material.* The extreme form of this view is that the teacher has no responsibility for the act of teaching because the teacher has no responsibility for the acts of learning. Partly true, but mostly false. The main aim of the teacher, in the traditional view, is to "cover the ground." In law schools these teachers are called the "lay-out artists." They are caterers of food for thought, but they have little regard for feast or famine among the partakers. They are the classic butts of the criticism rediscovered in every student generation: He knows his stuff but he cannot teach.

The system in the United States for preparing college teachers appears to make four to seven years of study prerequisite to knowing the stuff. And that is just for beginners. Postdoctoral programs (for further study), sabbatical leaves (of renewal), promotion based on increased knowledge—all are additional signs that expert knowledge is highly important. And so it is. Only recently have we become aware that one to two years of curriculum studies are necessary to analyze knowledge claims of a complex area for the purposes of teaching (see below, Chapter 4).

When one or another of the key aspects of each of these views is emphasized enough to exclude the other view entirely, a tension develops. Knowledge-centered teaching can become oppressive because it demands that the pupil conform to external standards no matter what personal pleading the student might wish to make. Person-centered advocates rush in to save the soul of the shattered student in the name of personhood, dignity, humane values, and even civil rights. Knowledge-centered advocates then protest the loss of objective standards and the sentimentalizing and infantilizing of pupils. The tough-minded and tender-minded fight over being right or being loved—the excesses in one view generating the other view, which when taken to extremes stimulates the original view.

Each sets a problem for the other. The problem for the knowledge-centered view is how to make instruction nonoppressive, how to make learning more like the development of personal meaning. Thus the concept of heuristic teaching, wherein students busily find out things for themselves, comes into being as a reaction to knowledge-centered views.

The problem for the person-centered view is how to keep the claims of one person from being oppressive to others with alternative claims. The problem develops with conflicts in views. When there are such differing opinions, the claim of each must have an objective basis, in order for each side to sample the other's views and decide whether trying them out is worthwhile. Such are the riches of person-person relations and knowledge-person relations that practical programs of education can long endure even though they oscillate between the two. It is difficult for person-centered programs to seek mastery of difficult areas of knowledge. These programs fail to see the liberating power of knowledge. Likewise, it is difficult for the tough-minded in knowledge-centered programs to seek the soft and seemingly insubstantial information found in the entwinement of complex person-person relations. William James wrote of the tough and tender-minded in philosophy and decided that it all boiled down to temperament rather than argument. He may be correct. As far as educating is concerned, I believe it is a matter of having an adequate concept of teaching.

These next two apparently different concepts of teaching are popular because in specific contexts each works very well. One context is that of *training*—in the laboratory, the field, the workshop. The other context is that of *instructing*—for example, by lecturing. In college teaching these two modes often seem to compete. Training is given powerful arguments deriving from vocationalism, practicality, the work ethic, specialization, and a no-nonsense demand for identifiable performances from the persons trained. One wants a well-trained airplane pilot to be in charge of one's own flight, just as one wants a well-trained surgeon to take charge of complex surgical operations. Less dramatically but equally justified are well-trained scientists, well-trained business executives, well-trained hotel managers, well-trained farmers, athletes, nutritionists, labor negotiators, diplomats, and journalists. The world of work demands training. The educational doctrine relies on reinforcement, operant conditioning, and behavioral modification as some of the procedures of training. It can be as successful as the range of incentives allows.

Lecturing in college also involves a specialized training—of the mind. Intellectual training derives from liberal education, and that education is delivered by the ancient art of lecturing. In the best lectures students are stimulated, challenged to think for themselves, and then left alone to work out the pattern of ideas for themselves. Such education begets self-reliance, the ability to solve complex and novel problems on one's own. Students understand how the life of the mind gives appropriate meaning to all other forms of human labor necessary to do the work of the world.

On both sides these beleaguered fighters keep each other going very much as two boxers prop each other up in the middle of the ring to keep the fight going. As long as the arguments are seen as competitive, the debate will continue unresolved. There is no way to settle the issue, because each side needs the other.

Even though there are differences in practices, however, there is no fundamental different in concept. The same arguments work equally well for both sides. Developing intellectual skills is just as much a matter of training as learning to following directions in a machine shop is intellectual comprehension. Careful thinking is a skilled activity, and expert carpentry involves careful thinking. There is no fundamental watershed between thought and action, only a variation in timing, quality, and context.

Discovery for Oneself

Some years ago, as an aftermath of the Cold War psychology of schooling, which made students into little soldiers of mathematics and science, notions like "Discovery Learning" and "Heuristic Teaching" emerged as ways to reduce the oppression of didactic, heavy-handed, knowledge-centered teaching. Heuristic teaching is a concept of teaching that deserves to be considered.

Dictionary definitions of the term "heuristic" include (a) serving to indicate or point out; stimulating interest as a means of furthering investigation; (b) a heuristic method or argument; to find out, discover; (c) (of a teaching method) encouraging the student to discover for himself. In scientific research the invention of a device that helps in understanding obscure phenomena would be heuristic. The device might be an intellectual construct ("neutrino" and "gene" had this status once) which helps in thinking about the phenomena of interest; it might be disciplined exploitation of a metaphor or mathematical model. If the device serves as the crutch it is supposed to be, it may be discarded at the end of the inquiry when one actually discovers what one is after. We see the parallel to teaching: at the end of an educative episode, the student may "discard" the teacher—that is, find out something through reliance on learned concepts and methods and therefore be free of the teacher. In addition to the function of heuristic devices as crutches, there are two other aspects germane to the concept of teaching. One is that heuristic devices are interestingly indirect. The other is that they lead to better understanding.

Indirectness. Many experienced teachers have found from their experience that direct (didactic) teaching does not work as well as indirect teaching. Knowing they cannot control the destiny of their charges; that they cannot *cause* learning that is good for their pupils; that it is immoral to make decisions for others which others ought to make for themselves—these teachers often subside into apparent indifference. But it is not indifference. It is a responsible indirectness. Since nothing is more boring than an answer to a question no one has asked, these teachers wait for occasions when the questions first emerge. One gifted philosophy teacher spent many hours with his class engaging in philosophizing *before* any philosophical term or labels were given; he wanted the event to occur, and wanted the students to see that the philosophical distinctions actually made sense of the event they had directly experienced. Socratic teaching has this quality of indirectness. While it may seem to the outsider that the indirect teacher is abdicating responsibility, actually it involves a readjustment of areas of responsibility—of the sorts of things the teacher is responsible for.

Better Understanding. Secondly, heuristic teaching has the important quality of leading on to better understanding. Much teaching is a matter of "from . . . to" From interest to knowledge, from a little understanding to more, from naive desires to justified and criticized desires, from facts to interpretations, from thoughts to thoughtful actions. Education in its progressive aspects is a matter of moving from interests, through educative episodes, to facts, generalizations and other knowledge claims, and values. An heuristic device can help in this progression. Like any aid, however, it must be seen as dispensable. It must not be allowed to substitute for knowledge.

Perplexing difficulties arise at this point. A teacher who tries to get pupils to find out things on their own is placed in a paradoxical situation: he or she is the teacher but does not teach; such a person appears to give up authority and special competence for the sake of having pupils find out something. The pupil is also placed in a paradoxical situation: he or she is supposed to find out something not known, but how will such a person know when he or she knows it? If the teacher just tells pupils they are right when they make their own discoveries, isn't that creating an unwanted dependency on the authority of the teacher? On the other hand, if they are so capable of finding out on their own and there is no need at all for the teacher, then are we merely talking about ways pupils have of learning, and not talking about teaching at all?

One way out of these apparent paradoxes is to view teaching and the pupil's development of meanings as episodic, as having a movement through time such that the role the teacher plays at one time is superseded by a substantially different role later.

If we think of educational episodes as having a beginning, middle, and end, the role of the teacher may vary. If heuristics are seen as helpful devices in the process of coming to know something, then in teaching episodes they can take on different meanings. In the beginning, the teacher might encourage pupils to guess, estimate, predict, anticipate intuitively. Formal proofs or established claims come later, as the conditions for them are better understood by the pupils in the course of their finding out things.

What is it we want pupils to find out? Presumably what the scholars in a special field of study already know. Then why cannot pupils simply read the results as reported in textbooks? There seems to be a conviction, held by many people, that when pupils actually do the work themselves—that is, recreate the knowledge the scholar already has—they have greater control over their own subsequent experience of finding things out. This conviction should be empirically tested. It is appropriate that we think about how scholars find out things. Discoveries are not self-certifying as to their value: that is, the scholar has a set of standards against which to compare any new reported discovery, and these standards are a function of the pattern of inquiry that generates useful knowledge. The teacher, then, is interested in getting the pupil to value the process of coming to know the truth in a certain area of human knowledge. Heuristic teaching encourages the pupil to try on his own to guess, to make mistakes, to see errors. By experimenting and trying, and making errors, he will presumably see more clearly standards of truth and accuracy.

There are many ways we can get people to find out things on their own. A catalogue inventory of these might be a useful research project. Researchers could interview a large number of teachers and ask them to describe ways they get pupils to make their own discoveries. Some of these will undoubtedly be objectionable. A teacher reports using sarcasm ("Oh yeah? What do you know?") to shame a pupil into doing some work. Another teacher is just ignorant or incompetent: the pupil decides that if he is ever to know about Cuba, he must find it out on his own. Another teacher provides a list of activities and directs the pupils to choose one and then do the work, but the pupil chooses a task for which he already has the requisite knowledge. Another teacher assigns a paper for pupils to compose and just tells them to go to the library and find out the answers there. Another tells pupils to do the problems and check their answers in the back of the book, but the pupils copy the answers instead of doing the problems on their own. And so on.

Nevertheless, just getting pupils to find out things on their own is not a sufficient condition to call some schooling activities "heuristic teaching." Suppose a pupil reports, "I found out that the capital of Texas is Houston." Isn't this the place where teaching, as distinguished from merely facilitating learning, comes in? Don't we expect the teacher to correct the mistake and, in so doing, to get the pupil to see the reasons for the judgment? The teacher helps the pupil to see the appropriate standard to use in judging a statement in geography.

A different role is played by the teacher toward the end of an educational episode. If teaching is to stimulate the heuristic attitude, it is not enough merely to give sanctions to correct pupil work. The art teacher plays critic to the pupil's completed art work in order to enlarge the pupil's understanding. The art teachers may say, in effect, that this quality is properly displayed in the work, that this other quality could be presented in a better way, that a shortcut technique might be tried next time, and so on. Similarly the science teacher who permits the pupils to mess around and make mistakes, to invent techniques for "getting at" phenomena even though the teacher knows of better ways, must let the pupils complete the process of finding out by determining for themselves what works and what does not. When some things have been found out for sure, the science teacher can still raise questions about how certain the knowledge really is, generate questions about alternative methods, raise appropriate doubts about conclusions, and encourage students to view warranted knowledge as a ground for a more refined attempt to get further knowledge. In this final phase of an episode, the teacher concerned with heuristics can emphasize the contextual nature of knowledge claims (the fact that the meaning of knowledge statements is partly a function of the context of inquiry which produced them), the limited generalizability of conclusions, and the possibility that different ways of viewing the same phenomena might produce an even more enlightened view.

Pitfalls

Persuasive Communication. The confidence man tricks you into thinking that you are going to get something for nothing. He persuades you to believe what you want to believe and in exchange relieves you of your valuables. The confidence man succeeds in establishing a belief system. He is like a teacher. He develops meanings, fosters illusions, creates beliefs. But the one thing he does not "teach" is the reason why his game works. He does not explain to you the variables he is manipulating to achieve shared meaning. The victim believes he has an independent ground for establishing meaning (the con man appears to be an inside operator who is on the victim's side, against an outside operator), the fact is that the belief is based on nothing more firm than appearance. Persuasions shape beliefs, and behaviors like teaching, but persuasive communication is not the same as teaching; it is an imitator of teaching, all the more deceitful because of its many elements that are similar to genuine teaching.

What is the difference? The main difference is that the effect on the person of the persuasion is short lived, and the educative materials cannot be counted on. The persuader must be omnipresent to keep the game going. In teaching, the teacher works to help the student develop independent grounds for beliefs, independent methods for testing beliefs, and checks to see when the student can make up his own mind without the help of a teacher. The teacher works out of the job. The work of the persuader is never done. As soon as one persuader leaves the scene, another may enter and work to persuade the client or customer to quite a different end, even though the means (persuasion) may be the same. A man may be persuaded that the car being advertised is a good one because a lovely woman is driving it; he buys the car, but he does not get the woman.

Indoctrination. This concept is so much like the concept of teaching that worldwide it is the method of education most often used. In matters religious, patriotic, commercial, domestic, and so forth, indoctrination is used to create the belief that a certain doctrine is so *true* and/or desirable that no alternative belief need be considered. Since Catholicism or Protestantism or Islam is true, no one need bother to consider alternative beliefs. Since it is "my country right or wrong," it is *my* country, no matter what people with different life styles might profess. Indoctrination is to belief systems as behavior modification or social conditioning (socialization) is to behavior systems. Both modes of shaping human beings are closed systems, and the person so educated has little if any relief or recourse from the system. Oppressive education is very popular.

Training. Training is not necessarily miseducative. It can be one of the good ways of educating. So close is it in practice to indoctrinating and persuading to a fixed end that the trainer must be very careful to notice the conceptual differences. Trained persons perform actions that display intelligence. These actions are skillfully performed according to a regular pattern or rule. Training resembles teaching in the best sense when the trained person understands the reason for the rule. Teacher and student work to establish agreement about what actions are to take place, and why *these* actions rather than others. Then the trainee is given ample practice until he or she skillfully performs the actions. Degenerate training begets actions that are performed well but mechanically: the trainee does not know why he is doing what he is doing. The teacher of the trainee must supply guides that permit independent grounds for the actions. In learning skills one must know the reasons for the regularities as well as be able to execute the skills.

The Key Concepts

I must extend the analysis of my preferred concept of teaching by looking at the different relations entailed by that concept.

There is a triadic relation (Gowin 1961) between teaching (T), educative materials (ABC), and student (S). I use "episodic" to denote the flow of meaning among these three elements in the triadic relation. In this section I shall discuss the content in triadic relations which makes them educative (contrasting the educative with the miseducative). Consider this diagram:

$$T \rightarrow ABC \rightarrow S$$

The teacher, T, initiates the action, laying out the intended meanings of the ABC materials for the student to grasp. The student, S, chooses to pay attention to those materials as meaningful and educative.

$$S' \rightarrow ABC' \rightarrow T'$$

In the next flow of meaning, the student, S′ (now changed because of some new perceived meaning in ABC) goes back to the ABC′ materials to extract and then relate back to the teacher, T′ (now changed because of the new information S′ has given), those specific meanings he or she has grasped.

In the next flow of meaning the teacher, T", may simply choose to repeat the initial giving of the ABC meanings, for instance, to alter them by paraphrasing or citing other examples, or the teacher may make a more fundamental move and return to the XYZ materials to retrieve a new set of ABC meanings to try out with the student (see below, Chapter 4, for further analysis). Another major move, assuming that the teacher and student have reached agreement about the meaning of the ABC materials, is for both to return to the XYZ materials and seek to retrieve new meanings for the next episode of teaching.

It is immediately evident that the triadic relation can be broken into dyadic relations. Some of these pair relations are degerate, some are educative. Educative dyads are those established in order to take a place in the educative triad. Degenerate dyads have become so self-contained that they interfere with the completion of the triadic relation. Dyadic relations are as follows:

Teacher → educative materials
Teacher → student
Student → student [teacher → teacher]
Student → educative materials

Teacher and Educative Materials. This important dyad is usually either overemphasized or largely ignored, depending upon the educative theory being propounded. Clearly a teacher must know something about subject matter, and most do, having spent years in courses of study trying to master a field. It is not so clear that almost as much time should be spent trying to master the materials of the field in order to reconstruct these XYZ materials into educative ABC materials. Scholarship and research that are devoted to creating the XYZ materials are not sufficient to recreate these materials so that they will be usable for educative purposes. This retrieval and reconstruction of primary materials into educative materials is the main teacher-curriculum task (see Chapter 4, below).

The degenerate dyad is easy to detect. Whatever the specific examples, and they are given many names, when the relation between the teacher and knowledge is exclusive—when it does not create a shared meaning as teacher and student come together over the material—the educative effect is degenerate. Some of the familiar descriptions of this dyad are didacticism, authoritarian expertise, giving instruction (where none is taken), lecturing (as broadcasting messages that are not received), the prima donna (so brilliant no one understands the performance), the obscurantist (so tedious and tortuous the trail of meaning, no one can follow), the detail demon (where the fretwork of footnotes is so complicated, complex, and trivial that the main message is lost). The interaction between the teacher and material may be stunning, but unless the dyad contributes to the triadic flow of meaning, the upshot will be miseducative.

Teacher and Student. The cure for the degenerate didactic dyad is often to give a prescription for teacher-student interactions. Clearly this prescription works well when teacher and student come together through the use of educative materials to create and share meanings. Instead of the teacher being on one side of the stage, protected from the people by a podium, the teacher and students are first brought together in order to know each other. There is nothing wrong with this move, as long as they are concerned to know each other *as* teacher and *as* student, sharing in the task of working with what may be difficult material. It is from the material that the criteria of excellence are derived and guide the teacher-student interaction.

Learners *cause* mistakes in learning; teachers can spot these mistakes and help set learning back on a proper course. Teachers cause mistakes in teaching; learners are often aware of these mistakes, but as students they often distrust their own experience and accept the mistakes of teachers rather than protest them. If there were more cooperation between teachers, teachers could help one another spot their individual mistakes. Videotaping teaching episodes helps to spot them, and it increases teacher awareness. In sports, mistakes and errors are part of the game, not something extrinsically imposed on the game. Mistakes and errors are not often thought to be part of the game of teaching, however, and few institutionalized structures are available to call the play immediately and publicly, as umpires must do in baseball. An explicit focus on mistakes and errors in teaching and learning would help tremendously in our attempts to understand and improve educative events.

Many examples of degenerate teacher-student interactions can be found. Teachers can exploit students, can make them become disciples by giving just enough information to intrigue them and withholding enough so that they are in a slavelike relationship under the teacher's control. Some teachers in college exploit students sexually, and vice versa. The intensity of this kind of personal relation will make almost any subject matter seem pale and remote. The sexual attraction (whether overt or covert) can blot out the educative concern. The common explosive bond could also be political, religious, or athletic.

For educative purposes a legitimate by-product of the teacher-student dyad is found in counseling and its many variations. Teachers often counsel students about jobs, friendship, sex, careers, and other immediate problems. Teachers should not take on these roles unless they have specialized knowledge for this kind of intervention. Even professional counselors are remiss when their services are based on uncritically held opinions rather than on knowledge. Academic counseling, advisorship, is appropriate because presumably the academician knows something about academics (though many do not).

Student-Student Interactions. Again, these interactions can be educative or miseducative. For far too many students the attraction of school is merely the attraction of their peers. Of course, peer relations can contribute to the triadic relation that is educative, for some students take over the role of teacher from time to time. Schooling degenerates into entertainment managed by students when peer relations dominate the scene for that purpose only. When schools are oppressive, however, it is easy to see that students may only permit themselves the humiliations of school because they have colleagues slogging through alongside. Peer values can keep classrooms cohesive, but in any individual classroom the cohesion can be bought at the price of education, not generated because of it.

Student and Educative Materials. This dyad is educative when the student is attempting to learn the material (see below, Chapter 5). Its degenerate aspects are very much like those of the teacher-material degenerate dyad. The student becomes a fifth-rate imitation of a fourth-rate instructor. The student uses knowledge competitively to beat down other students or to impress teachers, to get ahead by using knowledge instrumentally. It is degenerate when the student does not employ the materials using the criteria of excellence found in them. A student can fudge a lab report in physics instead of using the laboratory as a place to employ the criteria of truth-making found in the physical sciences. A student can write a well-composed term paper on "Floral Imagery in Hawthorne" by simply bringing together all passages having to do with flowers and leaving out all others; the paper may give only the appearance that criteria of literary criticism have been used. The paper may satisfy other needs: to please the professor, to pass the course with an A, to impress friends and parents. The crime of required courses in colleges is that students find ways to use their subject-matter materials instrumentally just to get through the courses. Once this path has been followed, it becomes apparent that materials can be used for other instrumental values as well.

T-ABC-XYZ. The interface between the teacher and the ABC version of subject-matter field XYZ is complicated. A primary activity found in this complex set of relations is the judgement by the teacher that the material selected will embody the criteria of excellence germane to establishing claims about the phenomena of interest. Most materials fail at this point. The snippets of information, the assertions shorn of any relation to criteria of method or verification, the interpretations grandly given without connection to facts, the bales of condensed paragraphs in the passive voice, the lists of names, the tables of numbers, the pages of graphs—all are unintelligible to the uninitiated. Often,

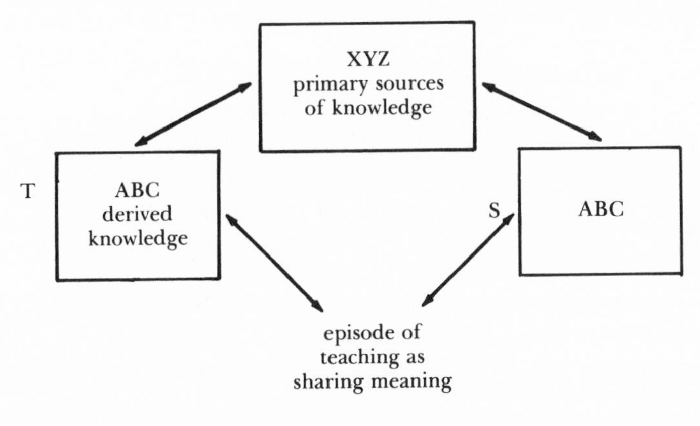

Figure 1.

textbooks in mathematics or engineering, for example, contain boilerplate mathematics, heavy and impenetrable; one suspects that the author put it there as a kind of secret code addressed to knowledgeable scholars or other textbook writers. For these materials to be transformed into educative materials, the teacher must crack the code: select, judge, try out, review, rearrange, refresh the course. This task takes enormous amounts of time and is never completed. No committee of expert scholars, no group of textbook writers, no set of departmental experts can really do this task adequately for every teacher. They can help, but each teacher should be able to master the material and defend the criteria used for the selection, arrangement, and pedagogical values of these educative materials.

S-ABC-XYZ. This interface between the student, the selected materials, and the world of knowledge is also complicated. Just as the teacher can be overcome by an overload of information unscreened by criteria of excellence, so too can the student be burdened by personal meanings unfiltered by the standards of the field being studied. The presented, organized patterns of thought and feeling and the immediate, idiosyncratic experiences in the classroom often can become a confusing mess. The student has a great responsibility for selecting, judging, reviewing, trying out, and rearranging the many conflicting and confusing meanings that emerge in a teaching episode. Meanings multiply for the student and, given many students, multiply again for other students and again and again for the teacher. These personal and pointed meanings are extremely valuable even though they are tangential to the linear progression of meaning represented by the textbook or the lecture. The student must work into this stream at some point. Just where and how and how well are functions of joint activity by student and teacher. The educative materials must help to make sense of the student's experience even though initially they often seem strange, difficult to the point of repugnance, and beyond reach. The student must not only comprehend the offered meanings but imagine how his or her experience *would be changed* by going beyond grasping the meaning and into the hard work of actually learning the material. To see how one's experience *might* be changed by learning is a rare and cultivated habit. We cannot expect immediate insights despite modern television, which appears to give them to us in various guises.

Next, the meaning of "episodic," another key term in the definition of my preferred concept of teaching. To think of the activity of teaching as having movement in time that is directed, definite, rational, and responsible is to complicate matters in the same way that gambits and the many other strategies of chess make it the game it is. The sequence is a complex of teacher moves and corresponding students moves and corresponding contributions of the educative materials. There are some patterned regularities we can point to, but we cannot identify causal laws. The path of educational progress, Philip Jackson wrote (1968), is more easily traced by a butterfly than by a bullet. Episodes of teaching are like the rhythms of Whitehead, the rhythms of romance, precision, and generalization. Even the complete act of thought Dewey described has its beginnings in indeterminancy, its development through various moves of thinking and fact-gathering, to a satisfactory ending: solution of a problem. Dewey's analysis of how we think is more like a series of episodes than like five fixed steps to be rigidly followed.

Let us return to concept, event, and fact. In any subject-matter field we find these elements. The pedagogical trick is to get students to experience certain events immediately. The handiest guide to making new and desired events happen is in educative materials consisting of records of past events. As records they are facts. Remember the threefold definition of fact as (1) the actual event that occurs, (2) the record or records made of that event, and (3) the summarizing statements and judgments made about that record and event. Another approach is to select concepts that point out regularities in events. A teacher may begin with concepts and use them to identify certain events that students can experience directly. The concepts can be used to make sense of the events as well as of the records of the event. The fundamental aim of the teacher at this point is to get the student to grasp the meaning found in the relation between events that happen (or are made to happen), the records of those events, and the concepts that can be used to think about and thus make sense of the happening.

One of the primary things a teacher can do for a student is to find a way to crack the code of subject-matter knowledge, the stuff we have been referring to as the set of educative materials. Music teachers do this for their students all the time. In various ways they point out what the notations mean, where the pattern of the musical piece changes, the spots the student may have to practice often because of some perceived difficulty, and finally what the musical quality of the whole might be like. When the student can make musical events happen by reading the score and find his occurrence directly enjoyable, then routine drill and extended rehearsal follow the value judgment of the student that these exercises are worth doing. At all times it is important for the teacher to check whether the work is so dense as to be oppressive or whether the student has the concept and the records by which to make desired events happen on his or her own. Educative materials are oppressive when the golden thread of meaning is obscured as a consequence of merely technical and formal requirements of the subject matter.

Implications

Teaching, I wrote at the end of Chapter 1, is the name for the initiation of an event using educative materials aimed at sharing meaning. The present chapter shows that the concept of teaching is complex, made up of many subconcepts and their relations. (But we will not have a coherent pattern of ideas in educating until Chapters 4–6 have been presented.)

In the triadic mode we establish one site, then the next, then the next, and use different tests for each, always seeing the threat of isolated dyadic pairs and seeing the need to keep the episodic flow of meaning between the three sites. The triad of teacher, educative material, and student develops such that each term in the triad helps to modify and give meaning to the other two terms. Thus it is not any relation between teacher and material but *that* relation of the teacher viewing material as something meaningful with which to teach the student. It is not any relation between student and material, but *that* relation of the student viewing the material as something meaningful set forth by the teacher and to be grasped by the student. The student must have, at some points in the episode, the power to ask the teacher to justify the material as something for the student to learn (that is, something meaningful and potentially valuable). Finally, teaching is not any personal relation between teacher and student (pal, counselor, authority figure, enemy, etc.) but *that* relation which makes each see the acts and bearing of the other with reference to the educative materials under consideration.

Teaching is consummated when the meaning of the material that the student grasps is the meaning (or sets of meaning) the teacher intends the material to have for the student. Educational episodes involving teaching are characterized by the deliberate finding, testing, and explication of meaning found in materials. If teaching changes the meaning of experience of the student, the student's subsequent experience will be changed also. The student's power to control better his later experience is grounded not so much in the teacher's authority as in the student's understanding of how the educative materials enhance and enlarge the range of experience. The teacher's responsibility is to see that what the student takes from the educative materials does in fact help the student in this increased understanding. A real test lies in the future: the way the changed belief systems and action patterns of the student do *in fact* enrich his experience. The line is hard to draw between the end of the teacher's authority and responsibility and the self-directiveness and functional autonomy of the student in the now enlarged capacity to control subsequent experience better. But the cord must be cut.

Perhaps the cliché of cutting the cord is too dramatic. Although teachers are metaphorically midwives, they are not attending a childbirth during teaching. Multiple connections are made and multiple severings are done. Imagine instead of a childbirth setting an educational setting, an episode, with teacher, material, and student interacting. The teacher has command of the subject matter—that is, mastery of the subject matter is revealed by the teacher's knowledge of its structure (this knowledge can be empirically tested prior to the teaching episode). Suppose we begin with what is often (mistakenly) taken to be the simplest element in the knowledge structure: a fact.

The student knows a fact or some facts. The teacher ascertains the correctness of this knowledge in some way and now wishes to help the student move on and discover more. One move for this teacher to make would be to ask questions about which concepts could be used to refer to the fact. The teacher can be indirect here, leading, probing, questioning, challenging the various concepts the students produce until at some point the connection between concepts and facts is validly made. The next step for the teacher might be to help students put the concepts together so as to invent a telling question, or a set of interesting questions. The teacher's greater knowledge of the conceptual structure of the field of study permits him or her to judge the difference between an important question and one that is mere piffle. The student may try to answer the question before they will reach this understanding. Hence, if the questions are clear, the next step would concern techniques and methods for answering the questions. Again, the teacher can assume the role of aide by refusing to tell directly the most appropriate and sophisticated methods of work, and by stimulating pupils to try to find workable methods. Next, assuming that all of the above is grounded and working, open-ended questions about the scene, the phenomena of interest, ways of conceiving of the universe, and the like can be entertained. Additional concern with the agent and the audience and with the kinds of values to be found in the area of study can be explored. Thus over the period of the educational episode, the teacher helps to knit together many things, including areas in which knowledge is uncertain, partial, or missing altogether.

Clearly a teacher and pupil need not always follow this path through an episode. One can begin anywhere. Progressive teaching begins with well-understood student knowledge and interests and moves through educative episodes into an enlarged experience of testing meaning and knowledge. Students may be interested in facts or concepts or questions or ways of working or any and all of these. A teacher who knows the structure of the subject matter can enter into the teaching act of any place, perhaps a different place for each student or small group of students. The point would be this: first one place gets firmly grounded, then teaching leads to greater understanding. The analysis of the structure of knowledge gives the teacher greater flexibility in choice of moves. The teacher's knowledge about knowledge helps him or her understand in specific pedagogical moves just what indirectness and guidance might mean.

CHAPTER FOUR

Curriculum

People climb mountains because they are there. They look at themselves; they admire the mountain, the material thing. In any human experience we may distinguish between what the experience is and what helps the experience come *about.* The distinction between person and thing becomes a mountainous watershed as we trace out the consequences that flow in different directions and over different terrain.

In my view, curriculum refers to a material thing which exists. Curriculum definitions which make the experience of the person basic refer to the side of the watershed opposite from my point of view. When curriculum is defined as "a structured series of intended learning outcomes," it refers, it seems to me, to experiences of persons rather than to the existence of material objects. When I define "curriculum" (below), I mean the definition to refer to curriculum *materials* rather than experiences that can be undergone as a consequence of interacting with those materials. I do not want one part of the whole educative process to be taken for the whole. I do not want to reduce teaching to learning, or reduce curriculum to learning outcomes. And sometimes curriculum is confused with administration, as prescribed series of drills and tasks are used by teachers and coaches to control the social scene of groups of students. Some books on curriculum are nothing but a suggested sequence of drills.

The task of defining "curriculum" is understandably not very popular among curriculum workers: the activities of making a curriculum are so complex, detailed, amorphous, and never ending that the central idea is readily obscured. Tasks are continually varied and constantly changing, one task giving way to the next without any apparent logical connection.

Perhaps it is obvious that "subject-matter content" is the main focus of curriculum studies; nevertheless, little attention is paid to defining what is meant by "content," even by curriculum developers most concerned with content. One recent curriculum movement is variously labeled "the disciplines approach," "the structure of the disciplines approach," "the structure of knowledge and the curriculum," or "academic rationalism." A simple definition is given in this chapter, and is backed by extensive discussion of related matters. One of these matters is a method for analyzing primary sources and reconstructing for educative uses the claims found there. Terms central to the method are defined and discussed: "structure of knowledge," "event," "fact," "concept," "value," and "claim." A large part of this chapter presents the "reconstruction of claims" as a major task of curriculum workers. A clear case of this work is discussed, and from the example a number of steps involved in making a curriculum are listed. The techniques of concept mapping are identified as a way of presenting reconstructed claims.

Among the most important claims of any field are the *criteria of excellence* the field uses. In science, two criteria often found together are reliability and validity. The reliability criterion is used to judge the excellence of knowledge claims produced by an inquiry by analyzing whether techniques of measurement pass tests of repeatability, reproducibility, universalizability. That is, one asks whether any scientist using the same measuring device under the same experimental conditions would repeatedly find the same thing. The criterion of validity sets a different task for judges of knowledge claims. A claim is judged valid if it refers to the piece of reality it purports to refer to, and if that portion of reality is thought to be important to the science. There are other criteria of excellence used by science, and some apply to scientific theories. For example, some theories are judged better than others because they are more coherent or more comprehensive or more fruitful in generating telling questions. Simplicity is another criterion for scientific theories achieved by concept reduction (Occam's razor—"do not multiply concepts beyond necessity"). Scientific criteria of excellence are usually grouped into categories for theories and methods. Perhaps the top two criteria are meaning and truth—claims should have meaning and should be tested for their truth value. What makes good science good is a fundamental concern of scientists and those who use scientific knowledge.

Let us take another example. What makes good literary works good? The criteria of excellence used in the study of literary works of art fall into groups around four elements—the work of art itself, the artist making the work, the audience experiencing the work, and the universe about which the work evolves. Thus, for example, the work itself may be judged for its internal coherence, the artist judged for imagination, expressivity, and craftmanship; the audience may judge by standards of edification and entertainment, and the criteria stemming from a concern with the universe include realism, accuracy, truthfulness. Different theories of literary criticism balance these four sources of criteria of excellence in different ways.

All experts in all fields employ criteria. One quick way to find the criteria of excellence in any field is to locate the experts, examine the cases they judge, and see how they use criteria to judge them. Experts disagree, of course, but they all use some standards of judgment and their points of disagreement often significantly illuminate what the whole field is about.

These criteria can be revealed by the method of analysis of claims. When found and explicitly recognized, criteria of excellence are extremely useful as explicit grounds for judging content. Every field is different with respect to these criteria, a fact of great significance. Questions about the "master subject" and whether disciplines are *fundamentally* different from one another (or merely different) turn on differences in actual criteria of excellence.

The Structure of Knowledge

The structure of knowledge, as a phrase in our language, sounds profound and important. The phrase is used by philosophers, epistemoloigsts, encyclopedists, and curriculum theorists. Many use it without precision, without definition. It is an ambiguous phrase. The multiple meanings it carries permit its users to misuse it, and in the worse cases to suggest a specious profundity. Even though we will not be able to prevent misuse, we should try to avoid it because something important is referred to when the phrase is used. I shall try to be clear about my use by giving a definition.

To begin, "structure" is a word that refers to parts and their relations. When we speak of the structure of a flower, for example, we name the parts and show how they are related. When we speak of the structure of a house, we refer to the foundations, the walls, the roof, and how these parts are put together. When we refer to the structure of knowledge, then, we expect to discuss the parts of knowledge and the ways the parts are related to each other.

The word "knowledge" is wonderfully ambiguous. Rather than classifying its various meanings, I will stipulate one of them. By "knowledge" I refer to the results or products of inquiry. I am concerned with what others have produced through research and scholarship. Academic knowledge contained in books, papers, monographs, research reports, and so on is the chief meaning I have in mind. I am not referring to personal knowledge or to the common-sense knowledge of the man in the street. I am referring to knowledge represented in primary and secondary sources. The structure of knowledge refers to these works of research and scholarship and to the parts and relations of the parts to each other.

When we actually take a look at these primary works, we find that this notion of the structure of knowledge does not take us very far. It is good as an orientation, but it will have to be made more complicated (unfortunately) before it can become a useful idea in the study of curriculum. In my early studies I worked out a definition of the structure of knowledge. It will be helpful to cite that definition here.

> The structure of knowledge may be characterized (in any field or exemplar of that field) by its telling questions, key concepts and conceptual systems; by its reliable and relevant methods and techniques of work; by its central and common products; by its within-

> field and outside-the-field values; by its agents and audiences (the so-called "community of scholars"); and by the phenomena of interest the field deals with and the occasions which give rise to the quest for knowledge. [Gowin 1970]

The first part of this definition is divided into five subparts. These five points have been named by my students as the Q-5, the five questions, because of the role they play in analyzing knowledge. I think of them as a method of analysis. The questions can be asked and answered in any order. All of them must be used because together they establish coherence in the structure of knowledge.

1. *The telling question.* What is the telling question of the work?
2. *The key concepts. Conceptual structure.* What are the key concepts?
3. *Methods.* What methods were used to answer the telling question?
4. *Knowledge claims.* What are the major claims in the work?
5. *Value claims.* What value claims are made in the work?

In short: What's the question? What concepts are used to ask the question? What procedure is used to answer the question? What answer is proposed? What value does it have?

Any set of curriculum materials should make obvious and clear this structure of knowledge. The simplest knowledge structure is the integrated relation between concepts, events, and facts. Such structures are very helpful to teachers for their many tasks of organizing knowledge for teaching. Such structures are also helpful to curriculum workers as they make decisions about which materials will be selected and which rejected. Furthermore, students in their learning grasp the idea that knowledge has structure, they experience the facility that comes with getting knowledge in this form, and they experience the fundamental base provided for subsequent learning. Students would learn to make events happen, to trust the records they make of these events, and to search for clarifying concepts with which to think about these events. Before these real benefits can come about, however, we must do the curriculum analysis and go the whole way from primary sources to reconstructed claims.

From Primary Sources to Analyzed Claims

Select a book, a research paper, a monograph, a serious study, or whatever you think is for you the primary source of knowledge in your field. Lay it on the table. We propose to analyze this document. To help you choose between several documents, use this criterion: it is a primary source if the authors themselves conducted the original studies. It is as if you are asking, "Who is the authority for this set of knowledge claims?" You expect to find the answer to be the name of the author of the work. Since knowledge seems to come from knowledge, as life comes from life, we seem to be caught immediately into a regression back and back. We do not need to be caught up on this logical possibility, however, if we can reasonably decide that the experts in the field would tend to agree about the authority of the author of the work you have selected. No matter how far removed you may feel from these experts, it is important to be able to trace your locus of authority back to theirs. There may well be a discrepancy between their claimed authority and your authority based on testing their claims in your experience. In such cases you become the authority and your knowledge needs to be made explicit so its structure can be analyzed. You will need to externalize your thinking in a form that can literally be put on the table. A curriculum is a material thing, a document of some sort.

Practitioners in the field of education do not very often work with primary sources. No matter how profound, basic, fundamental, foundational, or whatever these primary sources are, they are difficult to work with in teaching, curriculum, and learning. Their claims have to be reconstructed for purposes of educational practice. Otherwise we could just send children and students directly to the library with a list of basic readings and be done with the task of education. That plan does not work even for professors. The primary sources must be shaped for use in education. So, we have dual tasks. One is the logical analysis of the structure of knowledge; the other is the pedagogical analysis—the restructuring of knowledge for pedagogical use.

The logical analysis is simply asking and answering the five questions. But these questions themselves require some prior analysis. What is a telling question?

Telling Questions

A telling question is a question that is very good at organizing and directing our thinking, our inquiry, our sense of what is going on. As soon as someone asks a very telling question, others pay attention. The question collects our thoughts. It organizes our actions. For Eric Hoffer (television interview, 1969), a man not known for his scientific knowledge but well known for his personal courage and ability to do his own thinking for himself, one telling question was: "Why do the roots of tomato plants grow down when the stalk and leaves grow up?" Unable to answer this question, he immediately quit his job of packing tomatoes, went to a library, found a thick book by a German botanist, and tried to find the answer. He thought there *was* an answer, and that the answer was to be found in books. He reports how he persisted in his studies as a consequence of asking himself this question. For him it was a telling question because it brought together something he had never thought about before and it organized his actions.

Scientifically his question was not very telling. He did not have (indeed he needed) a conceptual framework, a theory about plant growth. Much of botanical knowledge is merely descriptive, naming (usually in Latin) parts of the plant kingdom; taxonomy-classification techniques are used to organize the names. Very few causal generalizations are to be found in botanical knowledge; consequently, very few answers to "Why" questions can be found. For scientific knowledge, a telling question poses a causal connection. "Why do the roots grow down and the stalk up?" changes to "What causes plant growth?" Explanations come in the form of causal relations between plants and light (photosynthesis), plants and gravity (capillary action), plants and energy (storage in the seed of linked carbon atoms, amino acids). Botany is not known as a theoretical discipline with much conceptual power; few telling questions are found there. With the advances in biochemical studies of plant life, however, the field is becoming more powerful.

Telling questions tell on phenomena of interest. They open events up to further search. A telling question is like a telling blow in a boxing match; something of consequence happens once struck. Like a telling point in an argument, something follows from it.

Linguistically, there is a tension in the phrase "telling question." It seems to be a combination of question-and-answer. If someone tells us something, we have a certain sense of completeness. We are told, we hear, and we acknowledge the complete transaction. If someone asks us something, we can receive the question but we may not be able to give the answer. We are puzzled, perplexed, facing an unknown with but a fragment of idea in mind. A telling question, as found in academic disciplines, is a question-with-an-answer. The tension between being told something and being asked something is characteristic of telling questions.

A telling question is not an hypothesis. The custom in much scientific research is to pose hypotheses. Hypotheses are hypothetical. Typically they take the form "if . . . then" "If I change this condition, then will I find X or Y?" "If nitrogen is needed for plant growth, and if I cut off the nitrogen supply, then will the plant grow?" The hypothesis is formed, then the experiment is conducted. These technical questions abound in scientific research. They employ some specific *technique* of research to arrive at an answer. The questions are *merely* technical in that the meaningfulness of their answers depends upon a larger conceptual framework. What often seems so complex and difficult about a science is the abundance of simple technical questions, specific techniques of research, and highly specific, limited answers. But technical knowledge is not scientific knowledge unless and until it can be placed in the context of conceptual structures.

Some Examples. For those who stand in a train station watching a train go by, the pitch of the train whistle gets higher as the train approaches, and falls sharply as the train passes. For those riding on the train, however, the sound remains constant. Are our measures of physical reality relative to the movement of the platform on which the measures are taken? Some version of the relativity doctrine has become a very telling question in twentieth-century physics. Most school children have heard of Albert Einstein.

Are there factors in plants which segregate and recombine,

such that visible structures expressed by these factors change from generation to generation? Mendel proposed his questions as laws of segregation and recombination. When he also proposed the mathematical expression of these laws as the expansion of the binomial theorem, he helped to provide a conceptual structure in genetics from which many technical questions could be asked and answered.

Is the superstructure of any society caused by the economic structure of that society? Most economists of the world today must try to cope with the evidence and the answers given to a telling question proposed by Karl Marx.

Is human behavior govered by forces in our nature of which we are largely unconscious? Does the unconscious exist? Sigmund Freud's theory of human nature and civilization and its discontents contains far-reaching telling questions.

Concepts and Conceptual Structures

Telling questions contain at least two concepts. To identify the telling question puts you on the way toward identifying the conceptual structure. By conceptual structure I mean the cluster of concepts and the way in which they are related. I have already given a definition of concept (above, Chapter 1). A concept is a sign or symbol that refers to regularities in events and in records-of-events (the facts).

Concepts, conceptual structures, concept clusters all come in a variety of forms. For example, the conceptual structure of music for the piano has a definite but loose form. This form has been influenced by many things: the historical traditions of music, changes in the concepts (of a scale: A. Schoenberg 12-tone scale, for example), the inventive grammar of creativity in music, and the four major traditions (linear, atomistic, holistic, analytic) for teaching piano music (piano pedagogy).

The existence of different and definite conceptual structures in a field of study provides us with the evidence we need to back the assertion that multiple structures exist in all intellectual fields: discipline is one word but many things. So, when we speak of the conceptual structure in our curriculum analysis, it is wise to remember that more than one such structure exists in any field. A historical review of the telling questions and conceptual structures in any field is a fine way to see these structures.

Concept-Mapping. Concept-mapping is a technique of analysis. We use it to show on a piece of paper just what a conceptual structure might look like. Once you have located the telling questions, or a paragraph that appears to contain the key concepts, simply *rank* these terms. Put at the top of a piece of paper the most important terms. Rank just below them the next set of related but less important terms. Finally, toward the bottom of the page place the terms that come closest to events. Draw and label lines of relation between these terms. When you have done that, you have drawn a concept map.

An Example of a Concept Map. Recall the text at the beginning of Chapter 2, pages 35–47. What would a concept map of that material look like? In the course of writing this book I have drawn many maps to clarify my thinking. Look at lists A and B and Figure 2. On the left is just a list of concepts in the order of their appearance. List B is a ranking given these concepts. Figure 2 is the map itself with each concept in a box, and with the lines relating them labeled. I have, however, added four concepts (teacher, curriculum, learner and governance) in order to present an overview of the whole chapter.

A. A list of concepts in order of appearance	B. Ranked concepts
educating	educating
habitual dispositions	eventful process
meaningful materials	change
criteria of excellence	meaning
indoctrination	educative
conditioning	miseducative
socialization	indoctrination
educative	socialization
miseducative	conditioning
deliberate intervention	deliberate intervention
refined set of materials	habitual dispositions
eventful process	thinking, feeling, acting
meaning	criteria of excellence
thinking	four commonplaces (teaching, curriculum, learning, governance)
feeling	felt significance
acting	
change	
felt significance	

A concept map is a very handy way to represent ideas. When a

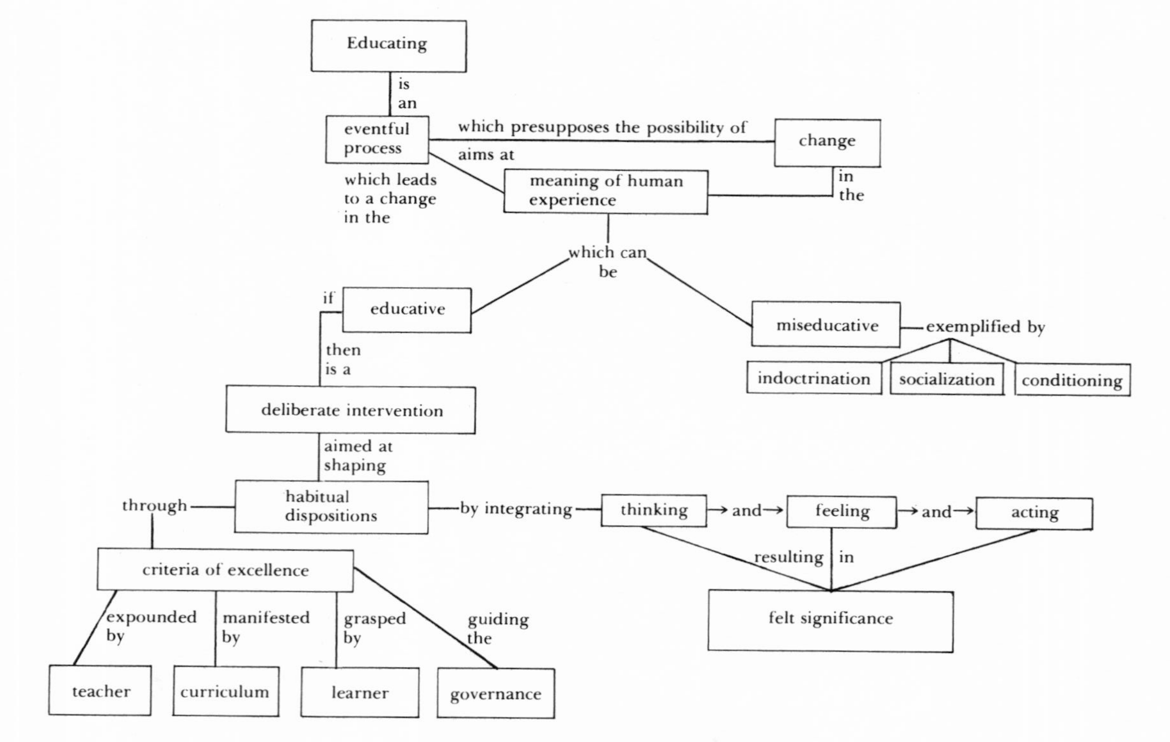

Figure 2. A concept map of Chapter 2

significant piece of curriculum material has been converted into a concept map, students can locate themselves on the map. They can spot the terms they understand and see how these are related to new ideas they do not yet understand. Students who have learned to use this technique can begin to draw their own maps. A concept map is like a rubber sheet; when we pull at one place to highlight one set of ideas we find that other ideas shift. No one set of concepts is fixed for all time in a definite hierarchy. The pattern of ideas has an elastic quality.

Concept Definitions. One of the most important things we do with key concepts in a field of study is to give them a definition. Defining what we mean by our key terms is a significant pedagogical move in making ideas usable by others. It is better, Charles Peirce (1878) wrote, to have a few clear ideas than a headful of fuzzy ones. Finding the definitions of the key concepts in a discipline (and knowing what kind of definitions they are) is a central move in curriculum analysis.

Some eighteen sorts of definition have been identified by philosophers (Robinson 1950). I am concerned here only with concept definition. Concept definition is similar to operational definition. The similarity is found in the relation between words and events. Basically to define a concept is to show the way the key term points to the regularities in the phenomena of interest, the selected events. Dictionary definitions typically define one word in terms of other words. At certain highly abstract levels of conceptual structures this word-word definition works just fine, but at some point every conceptual structure needs to be brought into relation to the real events, or phenomena, of interest. Getting an "event sense" of an abstract concept is a good step to take toward understanding it.

Operational Definitions. Operational definitions appeared in modern physics and philosophy in the first quarter of the twentieth century. Because there were difficulties with certain very abstract concepts (light, length), some physicists (Percy Bridgman was a leader) recommended that these key concepts be defined by discussing the way they were used in the activities of measuring. Thus length became operationalized by discussing whether one used a yardstick or the speed of light as the measuring instrument. In psychology, intelligence was operationally defined as what one does in giving and scoring intelligence tests. The record of the event of test-giving, test-taking, and test-scoring was the observation. Intelligence was then defined in conjunction with the operations used to measure it (Rapaport 1954).

Concept definitions are similar to operational definitions, as I have said. The similarity consists of the common focus on events and their records. But it is not necessary to *reduce* all concepts to operations as long as a connecting thread can be found between the most abstract of concepts and the regularities of the events of interest. Our technique for concept-mapping shows very clearly just how these relations between the abstract and concrete can be drawn in different studies.

Concepts refer to patterns (regularities) in events. When our concepts are well defined, it seems that the events are maximally invariant. The platinum meter stick on exhibit in Paris is taken to be the definition and the standard of precision for all meter sticks: its length changes very little. In ordinary experience most of us do not have any trouble defining a car as a car because even though there are many varieties (the variance is great), the regular features of a car (four wheels, a motor, gears, etc.) are common and familiar to us. Likewise, in the conceptual structures of a discipline there will be some concepts with precise definitions and others with definitions not at all precise. Precision and clarity of meaning are both important.

Concepts and Constructs. Conceptual structures in working sciences carry a share of constructs in addition to concepts. Constructs are simply ideas that help to hold key concepts together. These constructs are like bridges across one conceptual ground to another. They are constructions between concepts. In genetics, for example, Mendel used the construct "factors," which later gave way to "genes." These ideas did not have an operational meaning. Now that "gene" has changed, in biochemical studies of genetics, the word has shifted from a fertile construct to a definite concept.

Concepts and Logical Operators. All conceptual structures also carry logical operators. These are terms like "either," "or," "not both," "and" (meaning a conjunction), "if . . . then," and the like. These terms help in framing conceptual arguments. Well-reasoned arguments are a most significant part of any field's conceptual structure. In some cases these arguments can almost be reduced to logical forms (e.g., "not both p and q"). The closer one moves to simple logical purity, however, the farther one moves away from substantive assertions of claims about the world. It is important to recognize logical operators and logical arguments in conceptual structures, but it would be a mistake to substitute one for the other.

Concepts and Words. It is convenient to think of concepts as words. The word "time" and the word "tiempo" have the same meaning as a word. "Time" is part of the English language and "tiempo" Spanish. The shape of the words are different, and the sounds are different. Then what, exactly, is the concept?

First, words are carriers of concepts; they are vehicles of signs, as an automobile and a wagon are vehicles for passengers. But this analogy, helpful as it is concerning the carrier role of signs, is misleading if it suggests that concepts are entities in space and time. We should not try to locate concepts as mental entities in the mind, or physical entities of some sort in the brain.

Concepts are more like fluid events than fixed entities. When we think of words as carriers of concepts, we can also think that the vehicles of words (including terms, sentences, symbols) serve the role of concept facts—that is, *words are records of concepts* or, rather, concept events. We use words as the facts of language.

A word is a vehicle for a concept the way a token (a piece of money) is a carrier of value. We exchange tokens in barter and other free market activities. Words are the medium of exchange in free communication; we exchange concepts in a conversation. *In concept exchange nothing is lost.* One of the most significant points about exchanging ideas with another person is that nothing is lost and much is gained. A slight amount of energy is used, perhaps, but we scarcely notice it. If I give you an idea and you give me one in return, I do not lose my idea and I do gain yours.

Teaching, as the achievement of shared meanings, is economically very efficient (see above, Chapter 3).

Method, Methodology, and Methodolatry

A method is a procedural commitment. It is a way of trying to answer questions. The knowledge of method is "know-how." It is knowledge of how to proceed, how to get things done.

Some philosophers claim the experimental method of science is the most important method for making knowledge. They claim we have invented the method of invention, and that if a better method is to be found, the use of the experimental method would be bound to develop it. Other philosophers argue that there is no single scientific method, that science is full of different methods. Some of these methods are case study (clinical medicine), field natural history (naming and classifying plants and animals), observational (astronomy), survey (sociology); even trial and error is considered a crude method of empirical science. Mathematics has a special set of methods, as does philosophy. Literary criticism is an approach to answering questions about literature. Participant-observation is an approach of anthropologists as they study cultures and cultural life. Statistics has developed methods using probability and measurement theory. Historians use methods of positive and negative criticism in studying documents.

The insistence on only one method for making knowledge is what one wag called methodolatry. Such idol-making is to be resisted. We do become committed to our methods partly because methods are in themselves a procedural commitment, and once having found a good way to answer difficult questions, we are likely to become committed to that way, almost to a point of rigidity.

Methodology. Strictly speaking, methodology means the study of methods. When researchers ask one another, "What methodology did you use?" they are using the term loosely to refer to a specific set, or collection, of techniques. They are not talking about the study of methods. It is my belief that a study of methods would be productive. Yet it is seldom done. Occasionally an epistemologist will venture into these areas, and I hope more will become interested. It is a peculiarly insightful way into studying the structure of knowledge.

Methods and Techniques of Work. Techniques of work are the many specific ways of doing something. Using a microtome to cut tissues, and stains to bring out certain factors so they are more visible, are two techniques of work in biological science. Carbon-dating is a technique used in history and geology. Sampling is a technique of statistics used to make statistical inferences. Crossing plants is a technique in plant genetics. In most disciplines there are hundreds of techniques of work. To become trained in the use of these techniques is to become a technician. One of the most creative aspects of science, in my view, is found just here: the invention of new techniques. Even in cooking chowder, you need some technique to keep the soup from boiling so the milk won't curdle. Skilled doing is a fine asset in making knowledge. But: just why are we doing these things?

Making Records of Events. Making an observation in science means to make a record of an event. For example, to weigh yourself, you step on a scale and read the number the pointer indicates. You either remember the number (your memory makes the record) or you write it down (the written record of the event). Like the simple operation of weighing, almost all scientific techniques are ways of marking off events, making a record of an observation. Sometimes these records of events are called "protocols." I prefer the more generic term, "facts." Facts are records of events. Isn't that a simple, clear idea of fact?

Before we explore further the meaning of "fact," some comments about records of events are in order. Of any event we are interested in, we can make multiple records. If three qualified observers see an event, each one has a memory of that event which is also a record of it. Since memories are notoriously unreliable, we concern ourselves with other recording techniques. The devices that record sound, audiographs of various sorts, are especially important to human beings because of the limited range of our ears. Likewise, we see only a limited range of light waves. Except for the intermediation of devices of different sorts, we could not record radio waves or x-rays or gamma rays or cosmic rays. The devices—techniques and technology combined—vastly extend the sorts of events we can make records of. If there has been any explosion of knowledge in recent times, it is primarily the enormous increase in the number and kinds of facts at our command. Technique and technology are makers of fact. Fact is, of course, only one of the elements in the structure of knowledge. Extending the number of facts, like the records in the *Guiness Book of Records,* does not itself expand our knowledge of nature and human experiences. Facts are necessary but not sufficient conditions for knowledge.

Three-Part Definition of Fact. To call a fact a fact we need three things in relation. We need the event that happens (or that we make happen, perhaps in our laboratory). We need the record, or the set of records, of the event. And we need the judgment that the record we have before us indeed is the record of the event it purports to be a record of. Thus event, record, and judgment are necessary to the proper meaning of fact.

Fact has been defined in four major ways. Philosophers typically think of facts as propositions. To say "copper corrodes" is to them to utter a fact. But if facts are propositions, what sort of things are propositions? The assertion that "copper corrodes" must be further analyzed into the existence of copper, the action of the atmosphere on the copper, the sign (a bluish-green color) that the copper has changed. All of these observations require records, events, and judgments. It may well be that when we come to factual judgments, we come to a certain kind of "fact." And that is not in dispute if we understand what this judgment is based on.

Sometimes philosophers define fact as sense data. I believe the good sense in this definition consists of the requirement that some event occurs and some recording device makes a record of it.

The other definitions of fact need not concern us here. In general there is a tension in the various definitions between the "objective object which exists" and the "subjective observations of that object." The subject-object epistemologies all struggle with this problem. Our event epistemology puts a certain priority on the meaning of the components of "fact" as records-of-events.

Facts and Data. Data are facts that have been transformed. Typically, some procedure of measurement is employed to work with groups of facts. For example, computing the average is an arithmetical operation performed on separate observations of individuals (i.e., records). Statistical estimates of central tendency and variation are performed on observations previously made. I call these transformed facts, data. The verbal distinction (facts versus data) is important because it signifies the different operations used in "gathering facts" (i.e., making records) and "processing data" (manipulating the facts mathematically).

Knowledge Claims

A knowledge claim is a product of inquiry. An inquiry includes a question, concepts, methods, and techniques as constituents of the process that produces the knowledge claim. The knowledge claim is the answer to the question. Of any claim to knowledge that someone asserts, we can always ask them: "How come you know that?" If they say, "Oh, I don't know how it is I know it, I just know it," then we judge their claim not to be a knowledge claim. We should be able to get them to describe the question, the method, the event, or objects that the claim is about if we are to judge the claim as a knowledge claim.

Knowing is not the same as learning. Most people learn a great many things in the course of ordinary experience. Most of these "learnings" cannot be further analyzed into knowledge claims. We manage the activities of ordinary life with statements that carry meaning for us, but most of these meaningful statements are not the products of inquiry. Perhaps it would be helpful to distinguish between learning claims and knowledge claims. Learning claims could pass a simple test: Ask people if they think they learned, and if they say "Yes," then that is a learning claim. The claim may be meaningless, false, true, irrelevant, imprecise, vague, and so on, but we could still put it in the basket of claims that have as their characteristic that someone thinks he or she has learned. This basket will be very full. The basket sitting next to it marked "Knowledge claims" will be comparatively less full. Knowledge claims are a product of inquiry, and that characteristic marks them off from a large variety of other claims. All knowledge claims must be meaningful, but not all meaningful claims are knowledge claims.

Knowledge claims are artifactual. We consider art objects to be cultural artifacts. Houses, constitutions, laws, roads, and bridges, beds, kitchens, churches, games, and sports—all are cultural artifacts. They are things people in a culture have constructed. They are the product of deliberate making and doing. Knowledge claims are artifactual as well. Knowledge is a construction, a result of deliberate makings and doings. It is a fabrication of scientists, scholars, researchers, technicians, inquirers, the group of artisans who follow certain processes to generate products we call knowledge claims. The use of language here is worthy of note. The word "claim" suggests the possibility of error. The word "fabrication" is sometimes used to indicate an untruth. And so it is with knowledge claims: they may be subject to error and they may not be true. As constructions they wear out, are torn down, are reconstructed, are rehabilitated, are burned out, consumed, and transformed into ashes.

I am not asserting a cultural relativism, that knowledge is relative to the culture that produced it. I am suggesting that knowledge is relative to the pattern of inquiry that produced it, and further that knowledge is an artifact of culture just as works of art, technology, and so forth are cultural artifacts. It may well be that a culture with a slash-and-burn agricultural practice, like Haiti today, also has a characteristic mode of making knowledge. But the two, though related, are independent (at least logically separate).

Meaning of Terms Derived from the Context of Inquiry. A knowledge claim is relative to the context of inquiry in which it is made. The meaning of the terms in the knowledge claims derives from their use in the context of inquiry. For example, most technical terms (e.g., polypeptide, amino acid) are not found in ordinary language. All special areas of knowledge develop their own jargon. Moreover, the same word may be used in two disciplines and carry different meanings (e.g., the word "root" is used in mathematics and botany). If we want to be sure that our knowledge claims are meaningful, we will have to relate the claims to the context of inquiry that produced them. The process of analysis of knowledge claims requires us to set the context as part of the information required to give the "unpacked" claims meaning.

Generalization. A work horse in knowledge production is the generalization. A generalization is a connection-maker. It connects one event with another, one fact with another, one situation with another. The statement "All Indians walk in single file" is a generalization. It connects the persons with their mode of walking. If, as the classic story has it, one adds "at least the one I saw did," the generalization vanishes. One observation is not sufficient for a generalization.

The basic form of a generalization is "A case of X is also a case of Y." The most common relation between X and Y is a simple co-relation. We correlate height and weight, for example. We find correlations between the length of skirts women wear and war (short, during wartime). We may believe there is correlation between unemployment and inflation, between red hair and anger.

Correlation and Causation. A set of generalizations connects sun spots to weather patterns on the earth. The presence in our records of certain sun spots is sufficient to establish cycles of eleven and twenty-two years in rainfall and drought. It may be that the sun spots *cause* the drought. But at this writing the specific connections have not been sufficiently well worked out to establish causation. Any statement of causation is also a statement of correlation. But most statements of correlation are not causal statements.

Explanation. An explanation is an answer to a "Why?" question. In scientific work, causal generalizations are taken to be explanations. To the question "Why does the thermostat work?" the explanatory answer is that different metals expand from heat at different rates, and this differential expansion of one metal causes the switch to move. In analyzing knowledge claims in science, we give a high priority to the particular claim which provides us with an explanation of the events of interest.

Reason Explanations (Justifications). There is another basic form of explanation in structured knowledge claims. They may be called reason explanations or justifications. They, too, are answers to the "Why?" question. Reason explanations deal with reasons persons give for their actions. These explanations apply to person-events.

A common and ancient view of knowledge is to describe events—that is, to say what they are and what happened (make observations)—and then to try to understand why these events happened—that is, explain them. Aristotle is quoted as saying that "Men do not think they know a thing till they have grasped the why of it." Part of the structure of knowledge is the relation between descriptions and explanations. As we move up the right-hand side of the V (cf. Figure 3, below), we begin to see the connectedness between events, records, facts, data, generalizations, and explanations. At the top of the view should be *understanding* (interpretation). We want to know the significance of our knowledge claims. And that leads us directly into value claims (see below).

Understanding. "Acquiring understanding, which is what one gets as a result of accumulating explanations, is the highest goal of learning" (Scriven 1976: 217). Scriven goes on to suggest that understanding involves obtaining a mental grasp of *events*—that is, a framework of knowledge that spins off into practical suggestions, theoretical considerations, estimates of worth. An explanation gives us reasons by which to interpret the phenomena described and summarized in generalizations. If we accept the reasons, then we may claim to understand.

Thus there is a linkage of terms and statement forms:

(a) understanding comes from accepting the reasons given in the explanation

(b) the explanation is *of* the summarizing generalization

(c) which in turn is expressed through concepts

(d) which signify regularities in facts

(e) which serve as evidence for the argument
(f) and which are linked to records and events.

In a sense, the further we move away from events along this linkage, the more interesting the narrative becomes and the greater possibility that our understanding is increased. The amount of confidence we have in our understanding is a function of the tightness of the links shown by the V. If we can reliably move from one link to succeeding links and back again, we may hold our understanding with confidence. Helping others to reach understanding through clear relations of the structure of knowledge is a pedagogical value of the highest order.

Value Claims

A value claim asserts the worth of something. There are a small number of types of major value claims. Some of these value claims are directly involved in the production of knowledge claims (e.g., claims about the usefulness of a certain method, the precision of a technique, the clarity of a concept). Some of these value claims are less directly involved in the production of knowledge claims but are closely involved in the utilization of knowledge. A complete and well-rounded explication of the structure of knowledge in any area requires us to establish with some precision the exact relation between knowledge and value claims.

Of any document we are analyzing for its structure we can ask: What value claims are made? Is there a claim of utility? ("This research will be helpful in combating the spread of malaria.") A claim of social significance? ("All people who smoke should know that smoking tobacco causes lung cancer.") An aesthetic claim? ("A beautiful demonstration . . . An elegant proof.") Are claims of efficiency or effectiveness made? In what terms: cost, savings, change? Knowledge claims are surrounded by a host of value claims. The questions about their value can be answered by using a number of different standards, such as economic, aesthetic, social, moral. Typically, most knowledge claims are thought to have instrumental value (to be good *for* something other than themselves), and the most prominent instrumental value claim is that a specific knowledge claim is a contribution to more general knowledge (it is good for advancing knowledge in a particular area). Another prominent instrumental value claim ties the knowledge claim to its technological uses (indeed, many knowledge claims in Western science are not scientific at all but primarily technological).

The superordinate value claim is simply that the knowledge claim is *true.* Truth is the top value claim about knowledge. We use standards of truthfulness and criteria of the true to judge knowledge claims.

The next most important value claim refers to the *moral justification* of the knowledge claim. We may know that some given knowledge claim is true (e.g., the genetic code is universal; all living plants and animals have a genetic code; we can recombine pieces of genetic strips, thus altering specific codes). The moral justification for such claims typically is found in their *human* consequences. "What will happen to human nature if we tamper with genetic codes?" There appears to be no ultimately satisfactory justification for moral principles themselves (i.e., we can state the necessary but not sufficient conditions for moral principles). Nevertheless, it is part of our understanding of knowledge claims to see their connectedness (or lack thereof) to moral and social matters. As we move up the left and right side of the V of Figure 3 toward the very top, we are expanding the context of inquiry to its fullest boundaries.

The issues that *can* be brought in at the boundary edges can become extremely complex, vexing, and difficult to sort out clearly. Is science functionally autonomous? Is science in the service of the political order? the economic order? Should all knowledge claims pass a test of political correctness? What good is esoteric knowledge about insects when children are starving? Why should we know about the science of agriculture in Haiti when 90 percent of the people there are illiterate? Should we spend more money on basic research than on basic education? These questions are never fully and finally answered. That does not mean they do not *have* answers. Our understanding is improved when we see exactly what the answers are in any particular case. See Figure 3.

So far in this chapter I have discussed the structure of knowledge, primarily in the context of a method for analyzing that

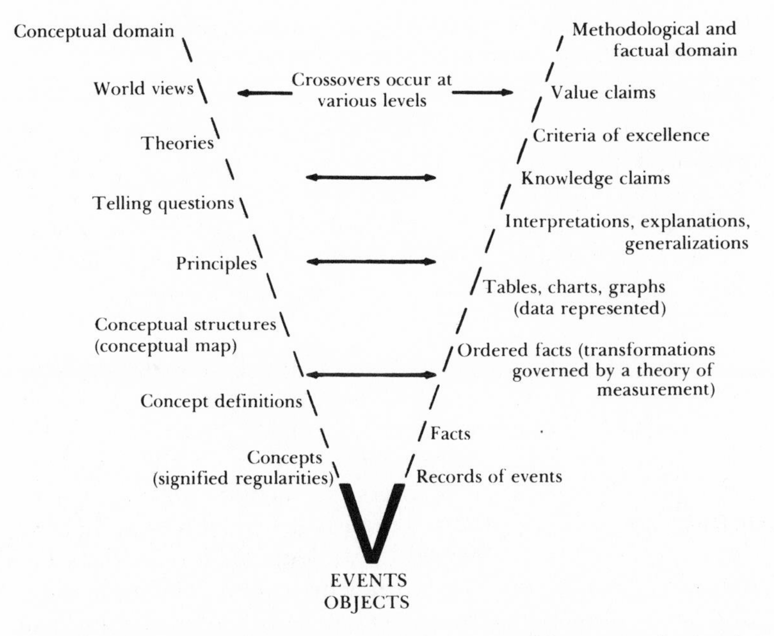

Figure 3. The connection between concepts, events, and facts seen as having the shape of a V.

structure in any specific field. When curriculum workers learn to use this method of analysis, they will be able to convert primary sources of knowledge into reconstructed claims useful in educating. Assuming now that our terms and distinctions about the structure of knowledge are clear, we turn to problems of curriculum. The problem of definition of curriculum is discussed, a preferred definition given and contrasted with definitions found in the literature. Next discussed are five roles of educative materials which follow from the analysis. The chapter ends with a discussion of curriculum inquiry and curriculum development.

Definition of Curriculum

In this section I do not intend to make an exhaustive and complete analysis of the view of other educators on the definition of curriculum. I do want to indicate the flavor of meanings given by others. I group the definitions into three commonplaces of teacher, learning, and governance to show the slippage from curriculum to other commonplaces.

Curriculum as Teaching. The alleged traditional view of curriculum defines curriculum as the subjects taught in school, as the course of study. Some claim the curriculum is what the teacher *uses* when teaching, that indeed the curriculum is what we teach. Some others claim curriculum is whatever content is used purposely in the school as a stimulus to learning.

Curriculum as Learning. A most popular view defines curriculum as all the experiences of the learner under the guidance of the school. Variants on this view suggest that curriculum is those things we wish children to learn in school, the school experiences through which learners may achieve ends sought by teachers, the school's program for learners, the lessons and tasks to be learned and performed by students, and as only a statement of what the pupil is to learn. Curriculum as learning slides into curriculum as governance in the view that curriculum is all the learning activities that take place under the direction of the school.

Curriculum as Governance. Stronger views of curriculum as governance are represented by claims that curriculum is all the experiences of children for which the school accepts responsibility, that it is the sequence of potential experiences set up in the school for the purpose of disciplining children and youth in group ways of thinking. Some claim curriculum is the school's organized program of initiating, guiding, and utilizing the experience of youth in order to build better meanings for the management of living, that curriculum is the organizationally planned and controlled experiences designed to educate students, or the planned composite effort of any school to guide pupil learning toward predetermined learning outcomes. Some see curriculum as the design of any social group for educational experiences of their children in school. The stress on organization, on design, on planned experiences leads to a concern with governance and control.

What I have called earlier the friendly old fallacy of changing the topic has emerged again. Instead of defining curriculum as something in itself, these various views focus on the teacher teaching, or the student learning, or the school planning and running things.

Some writers appear to believe that the school has purposes or the curriculum has intentions. In my view, this mistake confused things with people. People have purposes, but neither the school nor the curriculum has purposes. Schools or schooling may be a place where purposes are enacted, and the curriculum may be the material device that carries expressions of human intention, but the curriculum is not an event or activity, only a guide to such events and activities as people may choose to make happen.

My definition of curriculum can easily be seen as in contrast to the others cited. Curriculum-making is an activity; it involves many skilled people working over long periods of time, most of which time is spent away from the other activities of teaching, learning, and administering the school. The products of curriculum-making, including field-testing and evaluation, will, of course, reenter the performance of the other three commonplaces.

> Definition: a curriculum is a logically connected set of conceptually and pedagogically analyzed knowledge and value claims.

By "conceptually analyzed" I mean what is produced when one places the V on primary sources of knowledge. In that analysis we make explicit the structured relations from world views and philosophy down through theories and conceptual systems to specific events and objects, and then back up through records, data, generalizations, explanations (including techniques and methods), and value claims, including especially the criteria of excellence. By "pedagogically analyzed" I mean the concepts of teaching and learning and curriculum that are held while practical field tests of teachability and studyability are conducted. The feedback loop of information from these practical tests feeds into the last revisions of materials before they are pronounced ready for use in instruction.

Comparison to Other Views

Curriculum as What We Teach. In my view a curriculum is related to instructional materials used in teaching, but it is not exactly *what* we teach. The curriculum is the source of what in any given teaching episode may be used as deliberately selected instructional materials. One way to see these distinctions is to use the A-without-B procedure and ask: Can we have curriculum without teaching? Teaching without curriculum?

The answer is "yes" if the instructional materials are not derived from the analysis of knowledge and value claims called for in my definition. In actual practice most instructional materials are *not* derived from primary sources. A second reason to argue for the separation of curriculum from teaching is that actual curriculum research and development can occur in settings which, while they anticipate a teaching episode, are not at the time related to activities of teaching. Thirdly, if we think of curriculum as a guide to educative events (the record of prior events we use to make new events happen), then the curriculum is not the event; it can exist without the event happening; and the event can happen without the curriculum.

Perhaps the last comment is puzzling. How can we have an event of the achievement of shared meaning without the "meaningful materials" of the curriculum? The only answer I can see now is that the source of some meaningful materials used in teaching is not primary knowledge and value claims; the instructional materials used can be shown not to carry criteria of excellence; they are derived from some other source. For example, we can ask if it is possible to teach scientific knowledge without the knowledge claims used in instruction having passed the test of truthfulness? In fact, in practice it often happens; concepts and facts are taught without any apparent truth test connected to them. Is it possible to teach literature without aesthetic criteria of merit filtering the instructional materials? Yes, apparently so, as in the story of one English teacher who taught *Othello* as an answer to the question "Does a soldier make a good husband?" Can history be taught with records of historical events that are phony? Yes, in cases of indoctrination of political beliefs the alleged facts may never have taken place. Can values be taught without having been screened by tests of their significance? Yes, values can be presented in ways not connected to significant life experience.

In general we can have teaching without curriculum because materials of instruction can have meaning without further criteria of excellence having been used to judge their value. Also in general we can conclude that the relation between curriculum and teaching is contingent; no necessary and sufficient conditions can be stated to relate the two. These are practical matters of human experience, and they typically are contingently connected.

Curriculum as Learning. It would seem clear that curriculum and learning are also contingently connected. Learning, in the sense prescribed in Chapter 5, is an act of an individual to connect the new with the old and to work voluntarily to fit them together. The development and refinement of individual personal cognitive structure from conceptual structures requires only meanings that can be grasped as the basis for learning. It does not require tests of the excellence of the meanings taken for learning. Students can accept lessons and perform school tasks on materials having virtually no meaning—it is a fact that people memorize nonsense syllables. We all know that students can hold in short-term memory enough material to pass true-false, multiple-choice quizzes, and if they fail to pass, they, and we as their teachers, should know that they failed to learn the material because they did not connect it in important ways to what they already knew.

Curriculum as Administration. Curriculum and governance are also related contingently. We can have one without the other. For example, the curriculum can be used as a device of governance, as a way to control the lives and activities of students. Drills and exercises in the classroom, like those on the playing field, may have little relation to anything other than keeping people busy so they will not do anything else for a while. Sequences of group experiences can be planned and administered totally in the absence of any explicit curriculum because the experiences are only ways of establishing person to person relations (be careful to note who has power over whom). School authorities take responsibility for many student activities (e.g., riding school buses) which have no relation to a curriculum, overt or hidden.

Of course it is possible for a curriculum to be constructed with a proper view of its relation to teaching, learning, and governance: that is the point of educating.

Five Roles of Educative Materials

One is tempted to think of a curriculum as something one can literally pick up. A curriculum generally exists in some material form—as a text, a film, a program. A curriculum is an instrument, and it functions instrumentally. Educative materials are reconstructed from analyzed primary sources, and this activity is the analysis and reconstruction phase of what we call "curriculum." "Program" is the name for the organization of these materials in anticipation of their use in sequences of teaching and learning. "Curriculum" refers to the recovery of meaning from bodies of knowledge containing criteria of excellence for use in teaching and learning. Curriculum materials have at least five roles (or functions, values, significances). These five roles are:

(1) as vehicles of criteria of excellence
(2) as records of prior events used to make new events happen
(3) as the authority of the record
(4) as conceptual organizers
(5) as multipliers of meaning

Vehicles of Criteria of Excellence. Educative materials are calibrated instruments for use in teaching and learning. They carry with them the criteria of excellence we use to judge that they are what they are claimed to be. The difference between a book, say a novel, and educative materials is that the latter carries with it the criteria we use to judge novels as (a) quality novels and (b) useful for educating. It is not merely aesthetic criteria, or criteria of literary merit, that we need, although we certainly need these, but also the additional set of judgments about "educability" that we must have. Good art may be both pedagogically and aesthetically good. For educative materials to carry criteria of excellence, they must pass two major tests: one comes from the standards of the field from which the work originates and the other comes from standards of education. Curriculum analysis consists in bringing these tests to bear upon specific examplars.

Records of Prior Events Used to Make New Events Happen. The second role of educative materials is extremely significant. I am aware of no curriculum or educational theory that explicitly calls attention to this fundamental role of materials. Yet in one way or another almost all serious statements about education take a stand on this issue, at least implicitly. Part of the defense of the Great Books curriculum is relevant. Some scholars familiar with Harvey on circulation, Freud on the unconscious and Einstein on space-time could not believe that young people (aged 14–18) could comprehend these ideas when told to read them directly in the original. The defense was that it was like throwing meaty bones to puppy dogs. After the chewing is completed, one looks not at the materials but at the sharpness of the creatures' teeth. Like many other training materials, they were to be discarded when the educative event had happened. Training materials are like training wheels on a bicycle—useful in making a risky event happen, after which the aids to the event may be removed and the person moves on his own.

Consider the example of the music teacher marking up a musical score for the piano student. The materials are worked over so that the student can use them to make a complex event happen: reading the notes, playing them, and so on. The materials in their pedagogical form may be discarded as the student learns the piece of music, but the music itself as recorded on the score is not discarded. Memorized or not (the memory is a record), it is retained to make the "same" event happen again. We should look at how sharp our students are becoming by chewing over their materials. We do not discard the materials, however, as we would discard old bones. Old bones can no longer make new events happen; old materials can.

Teachers need to recover an event sense of subject matter. They need to think of the curriculum as records of prior events we use to make new events happen. Educating is an activity. It is in motion; things change; people use energy to grow and develop; it is a happening; as in physics there is a relation between energy and matter—when matter is dense, energy is slow; when energy is abundant, matter is spread widely. So, too, with subject matter—when it is too dense, nothing happens. Subject matter should release energy, not block it.

The Authority of the Record. As the authority of the record, curriculum materials can serve to reduce oppressiveness of educative events when only person-person actions are considered. If the curriculum is sufficiently accessible to a student, then, in case there is a conflict between teacher and student over who is right or what is correct, the student can appeal to the authority of the record. The curriculum can serve as a governing device for person-person decisions.

Conceptual Organizers. A conceptually organized curriculum can be of direct help to the thinking of both teachers and students. To the extent that key concepts and telling questions are clearly in the foreground, these elements serve as "advance organizers." They become the most powerful tools we have for human thinking about events and claims. Even in "slow-track" school curricula, the concepts and questions should be favored over facts (usually to be memorized) and routine descriptive information. A few clear ideas are much better for students than many vague ones buried in baskets of simple information.

Multipliers of Meaning. Another important role for educative materials is the increase in human intelligence which the materials permit. Each person does not have to repeat all of human experience to become educated. Selected materials are efficient; they help us get the point in an ordered, direct, clear way. We learn to comprehend a lot from a little. Like the multiplier effect Keynes wrote of in economics, the spreading of meaningful information through education is a real increase in human capital. It is not a mere brick-upon-brick, item-for-item, cumulation of pieces. Every time new information helps to reorganize the meaning of what is already known, there is added significance. It is the increase in new connections in the pattern or set of relations which *are* the new reorganizations.

Becoming educated is like the growth of a butterfly from egg to larva to cocoon to butterfly; it is not like the steady development of physical growth. The stages are qualitatively different in the butterfly; educational stages are also qualitatively different. Intrinsic continuity does not necessarily mean sameness. Progressive education, from the psychological to the logical, can change the meaning of experience dramatically as one moves from a strong feeling of involvement to a strong knowledge yielding power, mastery. Significant learning is the reconstruction of human experience as that experience changes, much like the change from larva worm to cocoon to emergent butterfly.

Curriculum Inquiry

The critical analysis of documented claims generates the raw material for making these claims into educative materials of the curriculum. We have discussed what analysis entails. What does it mean, then, to undertake reconstruction, to develop curriculum? Is development a legitimate form of inquiry? What procedures and activities (techniques and methods) are involved in curriculum development? What ideas (concepts and criteria) guide this bit of education studies? We will illustrate our answers to these questions with examples from a particular study.

Method. From Dewey's *Logic* (1938) we obtain one principle of method. Dewey claimed that reflective analysis of prior scientific assertions and the scientific methods that produced the assertions was a general method philosophers could use to develop a theory of inquiry. Dewey held logic to be what guided the conduct of inquiry. And logic itself was derived from analysis of what guided past successes and failures of inquiry. Thus we see again the back-and-forthness of the relation between the product (what inquiry produces) and the criteria (the logic that guides inquiry). I think the Dewey recommendation is apt for curriculum studies. We cannot limit ourselves to science, nor can we limit ourselves to one theory of inquiry for all studies we might wish to include in the curriculum. We can, however, follow the methodological recommendation. We can take exemplars from whatever field we are interested in and critically (i.e., according to criteria) analyze these products. From this process we can sift and sort until we come across products that appear to satisfy our criteria best, and we can choose them. We use the criteria of excellence signified by the products and the process of judging those products. I used this method in analyzing products of education research in the Millman-Gowin study (1974).

An Example. This study involved a small USOE grant concerning materials for the training of educational researchers and resulted in a small book. According to a popular pedagogical idea at the time, these materials were to be as self-contained and self-instructional as possible. Another fact about those times was the large cadre of educational researchers filling posts at new and federally funded research and development centers, educational laboratories, and information development and diffusion programs like the ERIC system. Thus the instructional materials could be for an audience somewhat different from the typical class of students in courses of research methodology at a university. One key idea, and our starting point, was that the products of research efforts should be used to guide educational practice.

The Steps in Making a Curriculum. Step one was a search through what initially were thought to be relevant prior works. We began by surveying existing guides to the evaluation of research. We found they had the common failing of not indicating with actual examples the criteria for judging whether an example of research actually contained the characteristics deemed important. The decision was made to develop a curriculum that would guide the learner through a critical evaluation of specific examples of educational research. The second phase of our search involved soliciting nominations of such research work from experts in the field, including school counselors, superintendents, college and university professors, and editors of American Educational Research Association publications entitled *Readings on Educational Research.*

Step two was the selection of prior works that carry with them the criteria of excellence helpful in judging the works themselves. We used both logical and pedagogical criteria in selecting ten articles that we felt represented a cross-section of research areas as well as research methodologies. Making our selections involved subjecting each article to a process of analysis of the epistemology in each product. (Compare the discussion above in this chapter on "unpacking" claims.)

Step three involved the reconstruction of a set of analyzed claims into some form of educative materials. This new form could be a text, a set of questions and answers, a module, a programmed text, a film, and so forth. In our study we drew on the analysis of the articles in preparing our instructional materials. These materials included instructions to the student, explanatory notes, assignments that focused on critical appraisal, questions, and, finally, model answers and critiques.

Step four required the use of the new materials in a situation where, it was thought, the materials would serve teachers and students. The pilot test was of the teachability of the materials. The judgments of skilled teachers were sought. Although student comments would be absorbed into the teacher's judgments, we did not, at this stage, seek to assess the materials in terms of what the students learned. Mistakes abounded in the first field testing; the materials had to be revised. For our study thirty college and university professors of educational research agreed to use students in their classes in research methods as a try-out population. Twelve institutions participated in the first field testing. Instructors were asked to withhold distribution of the model answers until the written responses of their students were received.

Step five was the revision. Comments of participating teachers and their students were helpful in pinpointing confusing aspects of the materials, but usually we could not rely on teachers to undertake the revisions. Sometimes radically new reconstructions were called for. We used responses of our pilot to determine (a) ambiguities in the questions and "model" answers, (b) places where it seemed necessary to cue students more specifically to the desired move, and (c) instances where further explanation was indicated. Revisions were undertaken with an eye to clarification and amplification.

Step six was a second field testing. This time we sought appraisals from students. We wanted to get from them some judgment of what they thought they had learned, how well the materials facilitated their studying, and what value or significance they assigned to the materials. This step was a test of the "studyability" of the materials—that is, a judgment of the utility of the materials in the students' process of studying to learn. In the second draft phase, students were asked to compare their answers with the model answers provided, indicating where they thought these answers were ambiguous, incomplete, or in error. They were further asked for a general evaluation of the article and its accompanying materials. At this point the senior authors' responses to our materials were solicited. Comments were received from all eight. Finally, a copy of the second-draft materials developed for each article was sent to the experts who had prepared an initial review of these articles. The experts' evaluation was positive.

Step seven was a final revision, which was sent for appraisal to the original authors and to participating experts. Sometimes the authors wrote new material for this final version. The curriculum was then ready for use. The Millman-Gowin study is as an example of what it means to undertake the analysis and reconstruction of claims.

Ideas that Guide Practice. We were guided by several principles. We had, for example, definite ideas about pedagogy. With respect to learning, we wanted the students to have the experience of comparing their analyses of the research papers with the model critiques we had constructed. We thought that students might learn something by reading, by thinking, by writing out their criticisms, and by reading our reasons for our own criticisms. Notice that we did not expect the students to learn what we set forth. Our concept of teaching is closely related to this point. If teaching is the achievement of shared meaning, the students have only to grasp the meaning of the materials to see the congruence between our meanings and their own personal meanings. Whether they want to go further and actually reorganize their own meaning structures is a question that is best left to them. In addition, our concept of curriculum includes the notions that primary materials should be made available to students, that expert commentary about these materials from both the authors and other scholars is necessary, and that the primary materials to become educative materials must be reconstructed in some way that draws together ideas about teaching and learning. Our concept of educating must be seen as a network of relations between teaching, curriculum, learning, and governing.

Another idea that guided this work was the need to establish congruence of meaning about each paper, a congruence shared by all the relevant parties: the original authors, the experts, the teachers, us as authors, and the students. If curriculum development is to begin with primary sources, the meaning of the original must be kept intact throughout the process of analysis and reconstruction—that is, the primary source of knowledge must be available.

A third idea we put into practice is the need for a practical test of the teachability and studyability of the materials. The practice of field testing derives from pragmatism—namely, that the meaning of verbal distinctions is secured if and only if distinctions in language make a difference in the context in which they are intended to make a difference. The very notion of testing materials in the field may be traced back to Charles Peirce, who said pragmatism was the "laboratory habit of mind."

Is curriculum development making new knowledge? Some people think that research makes new knowledge and that curriculum work is not properly called research. In the example of the field testing of our curriculum we could call the relevant parties in the field work members of a large curriculum committee. Ideally, curriculum research and development should include: the original author(s), fellow scholar-analysts in the specialty (the experts), the analysts of the original papers (in this case Millman and Gowin), the teachers who tried out the materials for their teachability (first field test), the students who tried out the materials for their study-ability (second field test), and, finally, those responsible for pulling together all the material to put it in book form. In our case, by the time we had completed the second field test we had involved over 800 students, 50 scholars, and teachers in 27 different colleges and universities. A large committee! The final product in curriculum development represents new knowledge as much as does an experimental research paper, and it is knowledge of a scholarly and practical sort.

Curriculum Development: Review and Implications

Curriculum development entails a focus upon the "What" in "What is to be taught?" Any primary source material can be analyzed into the three related elements of events, concepts that point to regularities in these events, and the facts as records and claims made about these events. In the subdomain of curriculum we see the central role of disciplined criticism as a method of study.

The curriculum worker is a paradigm hunter. In the past he has been dependent upon the specialists to describe their paradigms. He had to take the package as made up by the specialist. He could not pose his own questions and have the specialist answer them. Part of the reason is that the curriculum theorist seldom had epistemological questions to ask. He could not systematically analyze the structure of knowledge in the relevant disciplines. He had no method of approach to defining the variable "What is to be taught?" The content that eventually was selected for teaching in the schools usually got selected on nonrational criteria—of power rather than reason. Social claims, not knowledge claims, carried the day.

To make a curriculum means to undertake several related actions. First, one must identify primary source materials as candidates for educative materials. Secondly, one must find a way to extract the meanings of these primary source materials—that is, identify their elements and structure, including elements that constitute the criteria of excellence found in these primary sources. This analysis moves through the materials to the point where the key concepts, the events in the phenomena of interest, and the facts are clearly seen as related to one another. Thirdly, one must reconstruct these elements into their various pedagogically significant roles. To accomplish this reconstruction requires two notions: what the criteria of excellence are, and what is and is not educative.

What percentage of teachers can use the method of curriculum inquiry? Students of mine who have been teachers tell me that the method I recommend for converting primary sources into reconstructed claims is too difficult; I should not expect teachers to perform these tasks. Typically it takes me one semester of course work to bring graduate students at Cornell to the point where they can do these tasks satisfactorily. A lot of unlearning has to occur first, apparently. Some students are much faster at catching on than others, of course, and the twin techniques of the V and concept-mapping can be grasped quickly. In fact, when Novak's research team tried out these techniques at the junior high school level (Novak, 1980), it found pupils able to draw their own concept maps and understand the language of the V within two to four weeks. For scientists, who regularly make the distinction between theoretical and methodological issues, the V is quickly grasped. Often puzzling to experienced scientists, however, are the answers to questions concerning the bottom of the V. Often to focus on these questions is to clarify both lecture and laboratory discussions.

But to return to teachers. Can they be trained to perform these tasks? I believe that a summer's work would be sufficient for a team of teachers to comprehend what is involved in "laying the V" on materials. It will take much longer, however, for them to work through all the materials they need for a year's work. But over time there should be a development of skill and content sufficient for the task to become a regular feature of schooling. The pragmatic test remains: try it and see.

At this point, concepts that yield an educational sense of direction—concepts of teaching, learning, and governance—must be joined to the working concept of curriculum. As with curricular materials, it is from the clear cases of education with which we work that we find criteria for judging something as a case (or not) of an educative sort; and it is from studies of educative events and modes of judging them that we derive the criteria of excellence for education. Thus curriculum as a subdomain of education is tied directly with curricular programming, where teacher, materials, and students are brought together so that the educative process may work.

CHAPTER FIVE

Learning

Everyone knows what learning means. We are all more or less clear about the change in ourselves which occurs when we learn something new. Learning seems as natural and familiar as breathing or eating. Learning marks a shift in the quality of our experience as we move from ignorance to a state of knowing. Often after we learn something new, we change our behavior in certain way. We also may change the way we think, feel and act about things. For most people the experience of learning is not unfamiliar; we know we do it. Only sometimes does it become problematic for us.

Learning in the Context of Educating

In the context of educating, however, learning takes on a different cast. Learning seems to be the chief business of schooling, of formal education, of the social concern to shape oncoming generations to master the tasks of the world. For a great many educators, learning becomes the key concept, the main event, the point of the total enterprise. For a great many psychologists the whole science of psychology depends on the viewpoint one takes about learning; theories of learning serve the role of an orienting world view of psychological science. To E. L. Thorndike, to Clark Hull, to B. F. Skinner we give thanks for trying so unremittingly to find laws of learning. We now know that we need *not* try that route any longer. Like logical positivism in philosophy, theories of learning have left a deposit in educational thought, but it is not a deposit that draws much interest, because the principle is so small. The nativists, the behaviorists, the cognitivists all stand apart from one another because of the position they take on learning (and development). Unfortunately for the study of educating, the science of learning as practiced by most psychologists fails to conceptualize the problems of learning in the context of educating.

Every human being achieves a language. That effort of matching arbitrary signs and sounds to directly experienced events is tremendous. Among animals it makes every human a genius. It is a feat so transcendent and transforming that other feats of human genius look ordinary. Learning a language *is* a remarkable human achievement. But there are no scientific laws of learning describing universal invariance. There can be no scientific laws to describe what by its *meaning* is a changing, arbitrary, open, inventive process. The variability in the learning process is far greater than the commonalities. Regularities abound like the creatures in the oceans, but the irregularities are like the action of the ocean itself. Human events to which we have given the categorical label of "learning" are too numerous and varied to be captured in a psychologist's nomological net. Hence, though it seems that ordinary people know what learning is, the scientists do not. When we get right down to the events of educating, the concept of learning is not all that clear and precise. Neither common sense nor science supplies us with what we need.

Educative events are artifactual and mutable (cf. above, Chapter 1). They are deliberately set by human beings. They depend for their existence on the cultural patterns by which volitional agents relate to one another. Human learning is a cultural artifact: whatever learning may be as a "natural" event (its biological or physiological basis), its volitional control depends on agents who can take the self as an object. Of course, individuals in a culture may not have control over the cultural patterns that surround them. Of course, what is artifactual may seem natural. For example, it may seem natural that women work in the house and that men work outside the house. It is not natural; the patterns of work of individuals are artifactual phenomena of the culture. Learning is an eventful process which the learner *chooses* to undertake in order to change the meaning of experience for himself. As such it, too, is artifactual, culturally patterned.

Educating changes the meaning of human experience. Are learning and educating the same? How is learning one of the interacting commonplaces? Changing the meaning of experience requires causal agents, one of whom is the learner. We have already characterized the responsible role of the teacher in working to achieve shared meaning with students. Teachers, we wrote, are not responsible for the student's learning because the relation between teaching and learning is not a causal relation. Students are responsible for grasping meaning. Grasping meaning is not enough in itself because it alone will not change the meaning of experience. Some *work* must be done by the causal agent of the learner for grasped meanings to work their way into what it is the person already knows. Earlier we wrote that educating begins in midstream with people who already know something. It is the person's present knowledge that supplies the power for new knowledge to be acquired. For the person as a learner, two things are of utmost importance: what the person can claim to know, and what the person can claim to need to know.

Thus the problem of learning can be stated simply: to make connections between what is to be learned (what the learner needs to know) and what one knows already, Prior knowledge of a learner must become accessible to the learner. We use the same technique of concept-mapping developed in Chapter 4 for curriculum studies. The person draws a map of his own conceptual knowledge. Also, one can learn to "lay the V" on personal knowledge just as on other knowledge. These techniques help to make freshly apparent to the learner those points of prior knowledge to which the new knowledge must be attached. We are now ready to give a definition of learning.

Learning is defined here as the *active reorganization of an existing pattern of meaning.* This definition needs elucidation. I have talked about a person creating, finding, testing, and extending meanings in order to make sense of human experience and nature. I have noted the role of choosing to pay attention as a selective first step in grasping a meaning extended to us by others. Teaching as the achievement of shared meaning suggests persons working together over meanings carried by educative materials that serve as records of prior events—records we use to make new events happen. We must, of course, actively take part in being guided by these materials. Given, then, that all of the above is working, we come to a point where we have grasped a meaning that is new to us. The question before us is how to integrate the new with the old meanings.

An objection usually emerges at this point. Is it not the case that "grasping a meaning" *is* "learning"? First, we note that we take in meanings of all sorts with ease. We remember conversations without trying. We readily take in the words and sentences and paragraphs in the materials we read. We routinely find our way around our dwelling, our town, our path to and from school or work place. These actions depend on selective sorting of all that is to be found in gross events such that some are taken as the signs of next steps. Ordinary human experience is full of "grasped meanings" that facilitate living. The existing pattern of organized meanings, of language predominantly, facilitates living. Sign and symbol systems "systematize"—give order and meaning to—the flux of direct experience. These smooth coordinations keep us going. Learning, however, stops us. We must stop, look, listen deliberately. There is something new that is not only to be taken in, but to be coordinated with other meanings. The grasping of meanings is only a necessary (but not sufficient) condition for learning. We can grasp meanings without learning. In deliberate learning we act to reorganize old meanings with the help of new meanings to make a new pattern of relation.

The learner must find a way to make freshly apparent in his or her immediate experience the points of prior knowledge to which the new knowledge must be attached. Once the connections are made by the learner, then practice, rehearsal, drill, or whatever serves the learner's immediate purposes are legitimate ways to develop the *grasped connection* and to make it habitually usable. How far one needs to go with any learning is hard to tell. We are both better prepared and worse prepared than we know. Only the actual event of relying on a perceived connection can give us the evidence we need for knowing how strong the connection is.

The Learning V

The main activity of learning as an eventful process is that of reorganization. The active reorganization of grasped meaning involves us in a large number of different actions of integrating and differentiating. Let us place this activity on the learning V (cf. Figure 4).

The learning V shows us a way to use what we know about epistemological elements to think about what often are taken to be psychological elements. Caveats are necessary. Whatever the relation between the epistemological and the psychological is, it is not a reduction—that is, we are not reducing knowing to learning. At the same time we recognize that knowledge is constructed by people, it should not surprise us to find a relation between knowing and learning. Furthermore, and perhaps most important philosophically, knowledge is not the sum total of experience. Most twentieth-century philosophers, in contrast to classical philosophers, accept the point that knowledge is only a part (and a small part) of human experience. Perhaps the rise of scientific knowledge has helped philosophers accept the difference between knowledge and experience. There is much more in experience than knowledge, and knowing that results in knowledge captures only a small part of even known experience. Knowledge is always limited, partial, incomplete. Moreover, as adults we "know" things we cannot recall learning, and if we have any choice about it we would surely "un-know" those things (For example, anyone who has experienced vicious prejudice or raging jealousy would very likely like to "un-know" their knowledge of them.) A final warning calls to mind the miseducative workings of indoctrination, conditioning, socialization, and the like. What is learned under these miseducative conditions is not what I mean by learning.

Learning here is nested in the context of educating. Examine Figure 4. Note that the main arms of the V are related by the activities of questioning and the activities of answering. Questioning, like most of the verbs on the conceptual side of the V, works to separate things. Questioning is initially disorganizing; it unsettles fixed and stable claims. Perhaps we have here a reason why much of schooling practice has no genuine questioning in it.

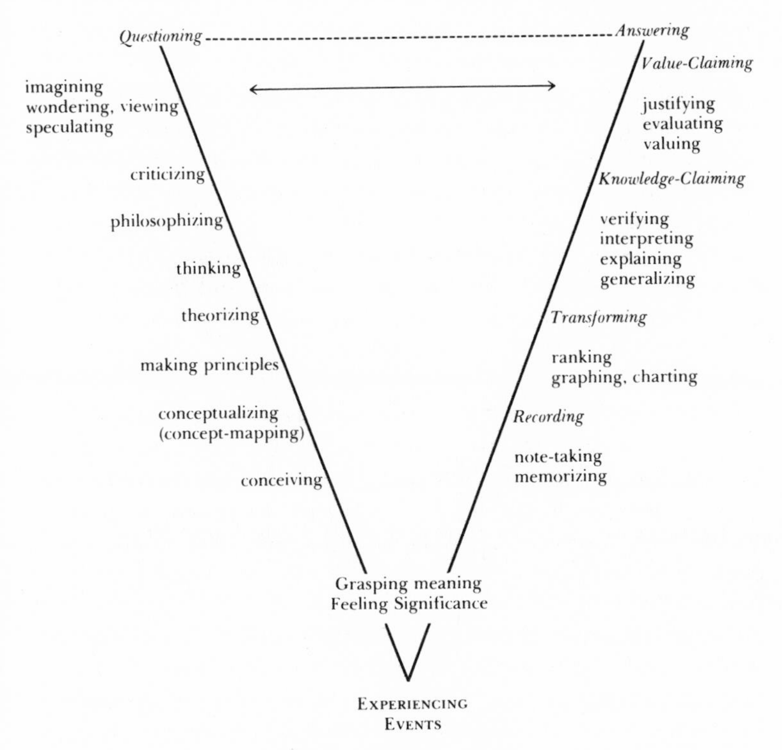

Figure 4. The learning V.

(Recently a teacher was overheard to announce: "When I want your questions, I'll give them to you.") Questioning, imagining, speculating, criticizing, philosophizing, thinking are all ways of separating things so recombining can occur. These actions pull things apart so they can be put back together in a different and more satisfactory and satisfying way. Answering, as indicated by the verbs on the right side of the V, works to organize claims in a definite and stable way. Much of school practice consists of giving definite, almost concrete answers. Perhaps boredom sets in as answers are given to questions that were never asked. The activities of recording, transforming, and claiming are ways of establishing answers. When the connection is made between a good question and its appropriate answer, we believe learning is possible. Learning in the context of educating is very much like raising good questions and establishing good answers.

In general we move easily back and forth between the arms of the learning V. We can begin—anywhere—with experienced events, with concepts, with factual answers; before we have finished we will cross over many times and move up and down, engaging in many different activities in order to complete our learning. Each side contributes something to the other; each level contributes something to what is above and below. In this discussion we will begin with the left side of the V and write a few words about each of the activities.

Conceiving. Conceiving is an act of identifying in the flux of experience some regularity, then giving it a name. Conceiving an event works toward stabilizing that event; it gives us a fix on the central tendency rather than variation, to use an image from statistics. (A jaundiced piece of folklore says, "Give a dog a bad name, and hang him.")

Conceptualizing. This activity brings several concepts together and expresses the connective tissue between them. Concept-mapping is an excellent technique for expressing conceptual structures. The technique is very helpful in learning concepts. When students draw their concept maps for a new piece of material, most find they make first one, then two, and often five or six maps before they are somewhat satisfied. This mapping can be rapid. And it is useful to keep a series of maps as a record externalizing the process of thinking involved in ranking, ordering, relating concepts.

Making Principles. The principle is a guide to the action of the event. In human learning, the act of making a principle is a conceptual matter, and it serves to call our attention to what is stable in events very much as conceiving calls our attention to what is common in events. These two activities of conceiving and making principles seem to be clear instances of learning because they indicate an active reorganization of meaning. They give us closure.

Theorizing. This activity relates concepts and principles so they are coherent. We may invent new concepts and constructs to bridge across to other concepts and principles. Freedom of postulation, stipulation, and definition are effective freedoms in acts of theorizing. The active reorganization produced by theorizing is clearly an instance of learning.

Thinking. In a sense all of the activities on both sides of the V require thinking. Learning is not a matter of mindless association (as stimulus-response associationists claim). Learning that results from thinking (in this special sense) engenders alternatives; it juggles possibilities; it shows how things could be otherwise. In the sense that we think with concepts, thinking presupposes conceiving.

Philosophizing. This activity is a persistent effort to think things through to assumptions, to presuppositions, to clarity of rational argument. The very limits of arguments are pressed and assessed in the kind of philosophizing which seeks the general case, the uniform example, the claim that requires "universalizability." The learning that results from philosophizing subsumes a wide range of concepts, examples, principles, arguments. Philosophizing pushes us beyond the coherence of theory to the comprehensiveness of philosophy.

Criticizing. This activity brings cases together with criteria. The critic examines a case in the light of criteria relevant to the analysis, appraisal, and evaluation of that case. Clear cases and countercases will test the aptness of criteria, and sometimes criteria change as a result. We have a bootstrapping procedure: from criteria we judge cases and from cases we derive criteria. The reorganization of meaning that comes from the activities of criticizing as one moves through cases and criteria is high-level learning.

Imagining. The use of the imagination in art is clearly required to produce a creative work of art. The new and novel in art reorganize experience for us. For example, suppose I am writing a poem: as the poetic product is shaped, words are added and taken away until a satisfying pattern is achieved. At the end, can I say I *learned* anything? Is writing a poem a way to learn something new? In the middle of the *act* of writing, the feeling of intense focus does not seem to me to be a learning event. Afterward, however, the creative act leaves me with a definite sense that I have actively reorganized meanings of my experience. I have learned. What a surprise lesson if a science teacher were to say: "Now that you've studied the history of physics, write a poem about it to show me what you have learned." Has any book on study skills included this suggestion to increase your knowledge by writing poems?

Using the imagination in philosophy is a working technique. We test clear cases by creating imaginary ones. Some books claim that philosophy itself begins in wonder. Speculating about the way things are and how they could be different—creating utopias and alternative patterns of meaning—seems clearly a part of the work of philosophy. And it seems to be one way of learning as well. Students of science who learn the philosophy of their science learn much more science than those who stick with science *simpliciter*. It is true of any discipline—art, history, mathematics—that philosophizing the subject matter reorganizes the content and thereby brings about new learning in students who study the philosophy. The reason is twofold: we add new knowledge (the philosophy) and the new knowledge restructures the meaning of prior knowledge. Scientific claims become nested in a philosophic content; we add a level of meaning and create additional intellectual space. Every subject has its philosophy; learning to a point of mastery requires us to learn the philosophy, too.

On the "answering" side of the V we find many activities that firm up claims. The "questioning" side of the V has done its work to the point where we think we know what would count as a good answer. The task now is to establish the answer. Let us examine the right side.

Recording. A clear case of recording in the context of educating is note-taking. Students learn to take notes as a way to grasp meaning. Sometimes, however, they take notes only in the hope that later on, the notes will have meaning for them. Recall the cliché about lecturing as the notes of the teacher transcribed in the notes of the student without ever going through the mind of either. A clear case of recording without grasping meaning would be a student's audiotape of a lecture. Students have to choose to pay attention to grasp meaning. Students who are grasping meaning during a lecture take different notes from those who simply make a running record of the talk. Note-taking can be an aid to memory. Students with excellent memories are to be envied. Students who rely on rote memorization for their learning are to be pitied, for they will put in a large amount of effort for only a small amount of understanding. When the material to be learned is not meaningfully organized, the most common student response is rote-mode learning, because the material does not have much meaning. At this lowest level on the learning V, recording can be sensible note-taking or strenuous memorizing. Becoming educated requires us to do much more than memorize, however; we must move up the V to reach understanding.

Transforming. Changing facts into data is an act of reorganizing meaning. For example, when we simply make a table or draw a graph as a way to present facts, we are changing a complex pattern of meaning into one that is condensed, ordered, simplified. These actions can readily be seen as possible acts of learning. When we make these transformations, we believe we can see something we did not see before.

Claiming. Making knowledge and value claims takes us to the top of the V. In making knowledge claims we engage in acts of describing, generalizing, explaining, interpreting, verifying. Each and all of these acts reorganize meaning. Similarly, in making value claims we undertake actions of valuing, evaluating, justifying. In establishing value claims we are, as it were, settling claims about the worth of something. These are marks of the closure of learning. In general, on the answering side of the V we engage in activities that generate "objects" that seem to us quite solid, reliable, repeatable, worthy—in a word, objective. When the crossing over between arms of the V ceases to hold our interest because our questions have been answered, we may say we have *learned.* Learning as an event has occurred. We have successfully reorganized a piece of the world.

Feeling Significance

Let us return for a moment to the bottom of the learning V. Feelings are very important to learning. They have a special significance when we consider learning in the context of educating. Out of the flux of experienced events we choose but a few to pay attention to as important for learning. Some events stand out because they arouse and express our feelings. They catch our attention because we feel they are significant. And sometimes it is the case that grasped meaning and heightened feeling occur together. In the example of grasping the point of a joke, the feeling of laughter accompanies getting the joke. Sometimes we laugh so hard we cry. These are very strong feelings. In the drama of a well-constructed tragedy, we feel pity and fear as we come to understand the hero's fatal flaw; catharsis follows. We feel the significance of the flaw as necessary to the working out of the tragic drama. If we did not grasp the tragic weakness, we would not feel the catharsis. Both humor and tragedy create events to which I give the name "felt significance."

Subject matter worth teaching has characteristic events in which feelings may be appropriately expressed: A law student should connect real feelings of injustice with knowledge about legal procedure; a student of nuclear physics who does not fear nuclear destruction of life on this planet simply does not grasp the meaning of his studies; a student of mathematics who does not feel the elegance and beauty of a well-worked proof is missing an important part of mathematics; a student of ethics should have a ready feeling for fairness as well as knowing concepts about equality; and a student of education who does not feel the hopelessness of meaninglessness or the zest of meaningful learning does not grasp the significance of educating.

The experience of significant feelings in the context of educating gives students reasons for choosing to learn. The learner with the help of the teacher faces the curriculum, shares meaning, grasps meaning, and feels the significance of the curriculum because the curriculum bodies forth criteria of excellence. Educative events are real events permitting an experience of value. Students and teachers alike should learn to look for these happenings. When they occur, they can provide a compelling motivation for the choice to learn. Such events are not thought of as coercive because the learner must have the choice to learn. But such events can be compellingly felt when their significance is fully understood. Learning, like loving, is not something we should expect others to do for us. Learning is its own intrinsic reward.

The Learner as a Causal Agent

The educative event is an intervention in the living experience of persons, and this intervention is designed to change the meaning of experience for these human beings (cf. above, Chapter 2). For the event to take place, however, we need at least two partners: the teacher who intervenes with the meaningful materials and the learner who *chooses* to grasp the meanings and learn them. In Chapter 3 we described the role and the responsibilities of the teacher. In this unit we shall deal with the learner as an active and responsible partner in the educative event.

Highly experienced learners, people we would called learned, know they are responsible for their learning. They undertake tasks of learning which require much effort. They work at their tasks, and their tasks are their work. Whatever acclaim they merit is based on sustained, responsible effort. They initiate tasks, and they are responsible for achievements. These obvious comments would not be of much interest except that in the context of schooling when it is conceived largely with inexperienced learners, we seem to believe that learning should be effortless. We believe learning should be "fun," "entertaining," "gleeful," "spontaneous," "natively occurring." Some believe with Aristotle that all people have an innate desire to know, which alone should be sufficient for the effort of learning.

Learning is a responsibility of the individual person. Each of us must do our own learning. We initiate a learning action, we undergo a process under our own control, and we complete an episode by knowing that we know. For example, think about learning to ride a bicycle or learning to swim. Remember the moment when you could keep the bike balanced by exerting your own power. These markers of learning are probably present in all learning episodes, even if less clearly demarcated from other moments in the process. We need to recognize them as reminders that human learning that is undertaken voluntarily is also a part of life that cannot be shared. Moreover, in the context of schooling in recent times, teachers have been held accountable for students' achievement. This practice puts an intolerable and impractical burden on teachers, because it is unrealizable. Teachers do not cause learning, learners do. If learners cause learning, we can hold them responsible for learning. The learner is the one who first chooses to respond to the event presented by the teacher, to grasp the meaning embedded in the event, and then chooses to work, to learn, to master. Choosing to learn is a necessary condition, but it is not sufficient: some other steps are necessary for the process of learning to occur.

The problem of human learning is idiosyncratic. Each of us must come to terms with our own specific ways of commanding attention, of holding our mind on a point, of trying and failing and trying again, or resting, of reflecting, and so on. Confronting one's ignorance can be *terrifying.* Remember when you first did something you were afraid to do? Was it swimming? Driving a car? Baiting a hook? Telling a lie? Hurting another person? Was it anything like knowing that you really did not know the difference between "their" and "there"? Confronting one's ignorance can also be *titillating.* Was it diving in the water on your own, not knowing exactly where you would come up? Was it jumping on a bike and just letting it go down hill? Was it steering the car down the driveway? Was it stealing? Was it doing someone in on the sly? Was it discovering strong but strange sexual feelings for the first time and experimenting? Confronting one's ignorance can be terrifying or titillating or perhaps somewhere in between, *but it cannot be avoided.* For most voluntary learning we must control our feelings well enough to yield our ignorance to the blandishments contained in the educative materials. Confronting ignorance and controlling terror can be an advantage if you really want to learn about yourself and about how you learn anything new.

In *Art as Experience* Dewey (1958) tries to explain what is involved in learning something new. He explains it by using the phrase "doing and undergoing": "Doing" involves deliberate action, like drinking a glass of water. To experience a work of art, Dewey suggests, we have to do something deliberately to perceive the work. We look. We listen. We read. We feel. We try to take actions that, in effect, put us in the best possible position to experience what the work has to offer us. "Undergoing" is less clear. Dewey writes that it is "controlled yielding that well may be intense." I have found the concept of controlled yielding very apt for thinking about learning. In learning something new, we somehow have to set aside our comfortable and habitual meaning patterns and try on a new set of meanings to see how they feel to us, and what they would mean to us if we learned them.

Several examples of this idea come from different fields. Readers are advised in approaching a new work to enter into the imaginative work with a sense of being led wherever the story goes. This imaginative projection into a new set of meanings is a controlled yielding. In philosophy, students are encouraged to get "inside" an argument or philosophical position and to see where it goes. Somewhat like a debater taking sides, the way into a philosophical view is to yield to its blandishments and persuasive appeal *before* one takes a critical and possibly rejecting attitude. To understand the argument in its own terms is an important precondition to appraising it. Furthermore, voluntary individual learning probably cannot begin until the person can regard the self as an object. Whatever age this is, we begin there. One must be able to treat oneself as an object in order to probe one's self, to see it as an instrument in learning. It may seem too obvious even to mention, but the primary educative transformation is the reorganization of person-centered claims with the help of knowledge-centered claims. Educational practice must be the practice of making the connection between claims of the person and claims of the material. This task is difficult, primarily because we have such crude ways to make accurate records of thinking, feeling, and acting. Our memory is notoriously unreliable. Seeing ourselves as others see us is very hard. A written diary is one record for ourselves, but it is not often very good as a personal record. In addition, various psychological mechanisms operate to disguise the feelings that are threatening or otherwise unacceptable to us. Psychoanalysis can proceed for years without satisfactorily exhuming as an accurate record the old "recordings" found in our childhood experiences. Recently, in the wake of the movement sometimes called humanistic education, investigators have developed a variety of techniques for encountering self and other people, and for heightening consciousness. Too few of these promising techniques also carry with them devices for making records of these prepotent events of the self.

Studying is the final task the learner has to undertake and for which he is responsible. Thomas Green (1971) has suggested that *studying is the task for which learning is the corresponding achievement.* I like this idea for several reasons. It points out that learning is a consequence of actions taken by the learner and not the teacher. It suggests to me that studying is an ordinary task of human experience that is not esoteric. We all can think of clear cases of studying. Actors study their lines, and an actor can be called "a quick study." A person who is in deep thought is said to be in a "brown study." A person who goes over notes before a quiz is studying notes. A person about to buy a house studies the contractual agreements. And so forth.

When parents and teachers give advice to students about how to study, they generally use a number of common-sense concepts, among them: (1) concentration, (2) mastery, (3) regular routines, and (4) working to completion to get a sense of the whole, (5) practice, (6) patience, and (7) exercise and drill. I propose to take up and briefly analyze each of these concepts. When all the old and new distinctions are put together into a conceptual scheme, the product will be a map of the domain of studying that is aimed not merely to commit things to memory but to understand how the meaning of experience is changed.

Concepts of Studying

Concentration. A common complaint of learners who have difficulty in studying is that they "cannot concentrate." They are distracted. The old advice about holding the seat of the pants to the seat of the chair gives us an idea of concentration but does not explain it. Concentration is the magnifying glass of learning. It brings to a common center what must be drawn together. Concentration means magnifying commonalities in events. To find what is common in events is to find a concept. Concentration, then, is concept formation. To say to yourself, as a student, "I must concentrate on these studies" is to say in effect that you must find the key concepts in all these matters. You must seek and find the commonalities. Other words for "concentrate" are *converge, center, fix, focus, collect, gather.* To concentrate is to find the key concepts, which are the kernel or nucleus of the matter. Students who are in the habit of seeking and using high-level concepts in their studies tend not to complain about an inability to concentrate. The key concepts work to focus the material and thereby help the students to concentrate. Those using high-level concepts just do not "sweat it out" as much as those who mindlessly memorize everything that comes down from their teachers. Nevertheless, even though we know what to tell students to do in order to concentrate, they must have educative materials that are conceptually obvious as well as powerful. The curriculum must cooperate.

Mastery. In recent educational literature the notion of "mastery learning" or "learning to mastery" has been linked with a notion (coming from evaluation) of criterion-referenced grading—meaning that a student will learn up to a cut-off point, a criterion. When that point has been reached—as determined by fair tests—the student can quit, go ahead, or turn to another topic. Criterion-referenced grading gives students explicit standards of progress, so they can understand how well they are doing and come to that understanding on their own time. They can, in effect, give themselves self-tests and know immediately afterward if they come up to snuff. In norm-referenced grading, the normal curve is taken as the normal distribution to which each student's performance is compared.

The ordinary meaning of "mastery in learning" is to come out on top in the struggle to learn. There is another ordinary meaning of "master." It is the sense of "master key" or "master switch"—the device or mechanism that controls the others. The master key opens all the doors; the master switch is the one to cut off before repairing another switch. The master key in knowledge is knowing how the several subparts of a subject relate to the whole structure. *To master knowledge is to understand the structure of knowledge,* to see the parts of knowledge which govern or control the other parts.

The two master keys are the conceptual structure and the methodological structure. For example, if a critic wants to turn off certain kinds of research in a field, the master key is method: find a fault in the method and you switch off all the subsidiary techniques of work the researchers in the field use. Another key is to find a fault in the conceptual structure. One major way to criticize conceptual structures is to show how and why the high-level concepts involved cannot be operationalized or cannot be tied to the regularities in the events they are supposed to be about. Another is to show that the conceptual structure, though internally coherent, fails to be related to anything significant. These are two master keys of criticism. They can become two master keys to studying. That is, a student should be able to trace the governing power of conceptual structures all the way to specific events. To get in touch with this connection is to find a master linkage. Additionally, the student should be able to see how methods of work and specific techniques of work are tied together and are tied to both events and concepts. To master a field of study is in part to understand these governing concepts and methods of work.

Consider two students in a science laboratory. One student moves about with the directions for the day's work, directions prepared for him by others. As long as the directions carry him (or her)—that is to say, as long as nothing seriously problematic occurs, progress is made. His coordinations appear to us smooth, freely flowing.

The other student looks hesitant. There is no list in his hand. There is a starting, and a starting over. Some arrangements he makes appear initially awkward. The look of thoughtfulness comes over his face. Gradually, as plans are developed, he moves with more confidence. He finds a way around apparent obstacles; the situation becomes intelligently reconstructed. Toward the end of his experience, if it is one of growth, he experiences a felt significance—a unity, harmony—of himself and the laboratory in which he works. Ideas and actions have become dynamically integrated; all the elements in a complex situation work in concert.

Growth in mastery makes the conduct of the student resemble that of a competent artist. Materials and devices are used, remade, invented to serve the purposes of relating concepts and events and records. Motion becomes spare, to the point, sure. From an initial tentativeness there grows a final surety. A finer, differentiated experience results. The finding and testing of possible meanings sums up with a reorganization of meanings. In the highest art, the greatest effort appears commonplace, effortless.

Regular Routines. Schoolmasters from time immemorial have advised students to have a regular time and place to study. Study halls and study times in schools are a common practice. But what is the reason? Is not regularity a dull student's crutch? Is it merely a parent's belief that regular study time will bring student and content together in the hope of learning?

"Regular" means formed, built, arranged, or ordered according to some established rule. "Regular" connotes the orderly, the recurrent, the *methodical.* We take our cue from the meaning of "method" in "methodical." Regularity in studying means to find and follow a method. A general method is composed of sets of rules and to follow a method is to follow a rule or several rules. To be methodical is not, then, to be dull and routine and unthinking. Just the opposite: following a rule is one good definition of thinking. To think carefully means, in part, to think correctly. Of course there is more to thinking than rule-following; set-breaking, for example, is a form of thinking very much like rule-breaking. (And I note here for further development later that "thinking" and "*learning*" are not the same.) Not all rule-following is thinking.

Regularity as a concept of studying means to find and to follow methods. *Methods make their own time.* Experimental methods in science, methods of quantity cookery in hotels, methods of house-building—all make their own time. To get a reliable hold on a subject matter through studying is to find and follow the methods of work that subject matter celebrates. A method of work should be seen as a reliable pattern of work. It is what we rely on to make the same things happen again. Some fields of study make their methods and studies of methods (methodology) most explicit. Other fields, like philosophy and literary criticism, seldom make explicit their methods of work.

The parental advice to have a regular time and place for study is usually well taken. But to find and follow a method will often mean that times and places must be modified. Clock and calendar regularity can impede rather than promote studying and learning. The reliability of a useful method does help to establish channels for the stream of our experience.

Working to Completion to Get a Sense of the Whole. A valuable asset in studying is to know just when one is done with work. I do not mean merely checking over the problems for technical mistakes or proofreading a typed manuscript. I mean having a concept of *completion.* I remember reading a classic essay by Isaiah Berlin on a problem of interest to historians. After reading for a while I noted the recurrent use of capital letters to mark off portions of the essay; they seemed to be in alphabetical order. I checked the beginning and guessed the end: he had exactly twenty-six sections, duly lettered. When he got to the letter "Z," he was well and truly through.

In this concept of studying, a sense of the whole to be learned can help greatly to give one a sense of sanity. There are "chunks" to learning and remembering. George Miller calculates about five to seven pieces for most people at any one time. Rule for the student: if you do not know the connection between the beginning and the ending of the subject matter, ASK. The familiar question "How long should this paper be?" is a distress signal. It means that the teacher and the student have not reached agreement about the sense of the whole. Without that agreement, how can a student know when the job is completed?

This brief presentation of ordinary terms may seem banal. There is nothing insignificant, however, about the power that comes to students when the end is in sight, when a legitimate sense of the whole is perceived, when a test of the comprehensiveness and completeness of studies is explicit and readily available to them.

Practice. Perhaps the oldest cliché in this collection of common-sense concepts is "practice makes perfect." Like many slogans, the meaning and use of the phrase are chronically ambiguous. In one meaning, practice implies something that is put into practice. We sometimes speak about putting a theory into practice; we speak of a dentist going into practice. Although there is something to be learned by the action of putting something into pracitce, the presupposition is that something is known *before* it is put into practice.

Another meaning of practice implies repeated performances for purposes of learning or acquiring proficiency. Daily flute practice makes improved performance more likely. To perform some action repeatedly in order to learn implies that we have grasped a meaning sufficiently well to repeat the same thing. We are using a set of signs to point to the same event. Learning through errors and mistakes implies some standard of correctness against which the mistake is "measured." Put differently, we need to have some way to recognize the event as *the* event we want to occur, in order to recognize mistakes for what they are.

Aristotle is reported to have said that one can learn to play the flute well through practice and one can learn to play the flute badly through practice. Repetition may improve skills if the player knows what a good performance is and tries to achieve one, but mere repetition of unthinking actions may seal in the mistakes and make for a poor performance.

The best practice, in studying and elsewhere, involves a basis of knowledge and a test of what has been achieved following the practice. One must know why one is practicing and also must be able to study the effect of practice so as to compare it with one's previous state of "performance."

Patience. Fatigue is a concept found in learning research. Patience is a concept found in self-management. The management of life's small and large problems can lead to fatigue and can require patience. Sewing, cooking, following directions on a do-it-yourself kit, rehearsing music, laboring to clean house—all are practical activities requiring a level of skilled behavior. Some times a person is better at doing these things than at other times. There may be no new learning in making a soufflé or in planting seeds or cutting grass, yet there are surely times when we need to do such things over, to practice them, in order to recapture the touch at the level of competence we used to have. Refining our sense of touch is to fine tune an ordinary task, and to make completing it seem to require excellence rather than mere diligence. The management of patience in routine learning tasks is required, and may elevate the inescapable drudgery of routines leading to mastery and excellence. Patience is indeed a virtue.

Exercise and Drill. Drill, as in spelling drills, has a place in a concept of studying. Drill is usually disciplined *group* training based on constant repetition and correction of mistakes. A drill is like an exercise in gymnastics. One runs through a drill (as in a squad) and one runs through warm-up exercises. There is nothing new in these matters. Efficiency may increase. A drill is an action that moves learning in the direction of *overlearning*. When one wants automatic and unthinking behavior, nothing better can be recommended than drilling to the point of automatic responses. Children, for example, who often have difficulty putting up their left hand or their right hand upon command, nevertheless do have the concept of "handedness" or "left-right"; they just need drill to the point of not having to think about what they are doing. One does not learn concepts through drill, for drill presupposes conceptual understanding. Confusing conceptual understanding with drilling is a pedagogical mistake. Conceptual learning is coming to grasp a new concept in order to think new thoughts. Drill presupposes that the thoughts are clear; it is the doing that needs to be made automatic.

Review and Implications

In this chapter I have so far presented my preferred view of learning and studying. Whole books have been written on these topics. I have made no attempt to review the literature, and may therefore appear to be discounting it. There are two reasons for thinking that this literature does indeed not count, or should not be counted on.

The first is that presenting a preferred view in the light of other views can distort the preferred view. To relate multiple views requires finding a common language to relate them. You often find yourself using the terminology of others to express their view, and then you must force your own view into that frame of reference. There will be ample time for making comparative studies when my preferred view has had a chance to generate its own data and audience.

The second reason concerns what I have called the fallacy of changing the subject. Studies of human learning often turn out to be studies of other things: nonsense syllables, maze-running rats, conditioning pigeons without a cerebral cortex, perception. These studies are about something other than human learning in the context of educational practice. Pulling habits out of rats *was* an illusion. Almost all recent empirical studies about learning in a school setting are subject-matter neutral, and the curriculum is irrelevant to both Skinnerian and Rogerian approaches. Studies of the behaviorists and the humanists which share this deficiency must be discounted. *What* is set out to be learned (the subject matter) does make a significant difference in an educational theory.

More recent work by my colleague Joseph Novak and his students impresses me as being on the right track. Using concepts of meaningful learning developed by D. Ausubel, Novak (1977) has produced studies of students learning science concepts that could fit the notions of meaning and learning which I have developed here. (See Bibliography)

I wrote at the outset that the most important thing about a student as a learner is what the student can claim. I believe that view to have substantial merit for pedagogy. Nevertheless, we find ourselves without too much knowledge about or familiar practice with making student claims clearly evident. Teachers need to find ways to probe claims. Students even more than teachers need to find ways to know what they know and what they need to know. The conceptual scheme of studying which I have presented may help students to get their voluntary learning under the control of their own concepts and methods. Undoubtedly other features of this large-scale map of studying will emerge as my point of view is used and tested.

Learning and Curriculum

Learning what? Sometimes theories of learning make assertions about learning as if *what* was being learned made no difference. The learning of nonsense syllables is thought to be no different from learning a poem or an algebraic problem. In my view we must pay special attention to learning in the context of curriculum. Chapter 4 above distinguishes the many different parts in the structure of knowledge. Thus, for example, facts were defined as records of events, concepts as signifying regularities in events, and so forth. It is important to observe that the meaning of facts and concepts makes a difference to our learning them. When we try to learn a fact, we act differently from what we do in learning concepts. Let us see how this point might work out.

In trying to learn a novel concept, the student's task is to connect a regularity in an event to the concept used to identify that regularity. The student works back and forth between the "language" about the event and the experience of the event. One can begin with either concept or event. Starting with a concept, the learner is trying to *operationalize* the concept. That is, the learner is trying to make an event happen (if that is possible in this case) such that a sign-symbol is "fitted to" events. The student's purpose is to undergo these events, asking, in effect, "What operations or actions do I perform in order to sense the pattern in the events to which the concept refers?" If a student is trying to learn the meaning of "photosynthesis" or "probability" or "entropy" or whatever, some things need to happen in such a way that the student can see how the concepts stand for certain regularities in events. A laboratory science is an appropriate place for students to undergo experiences such that regularities are tied to concepts. In philosophy studies, modern philosophers often begin with clear cases, counterexamples, imaginary cases, or borderline cases as ways to relate event and concept. Working out the principle in the context of examples is very important to conceptual learning. Students cope with excessive richness of cases and examples by sorting concepts. Some concepts lead to other concepts until conceptual structures, theories, even whole philosophies are tied together. Not *all* of our concepts can be "operationalized," but certain key concepts must be tied down to events as a basis for giving meaning to a batch of other concepts that are not directly experiential. Concept-mapping techniques show us these relationships.

A caveat is in order. Not all concepts can be experienced directly. We require mediators. We require meaning. Our language itself can be recognized for its power in mediating meaning. One piece of language recommends itself to us as exceptionally powerful in reorganizing conceptual meaning—namely, metaphors. The interaction view of metaphor (Richards 1936) characterizes metaphors as interactive as one part of the metaphor "tells on" the other part, and that "telling" rebounds to the first part. Let us take an example.

Learning Concepts: Metaphor

"Marriage is a zero-sum game." is a quotation which Max Black uses as an example of metaphor (Black 1977). The principal subject, "marriage" is brought together in the metaphor with the subsidiary subject, "zero-sum game" in a way in which each suggests something about the other. Black writes: "The metaphor selects, emphasizes, suppresses, and organizes features of its principal subject by implying statements about it that normally apply to the subsidiary subject" (Black 1962: 44–45). A consequence of an apt metaphor is that it provokes thought. In my terms, metaphors do this because they rearrange commonalities in events, and they bring the shared features of one event to bear upon the pattern found in another event. Thus concepts are joined. New connections are made. Meanings are reorganized. Rethinking occurs.

Black maintains that metaphors are "conceptual archetypes." They are basic ideas that subsume other ideas. To understand the new meanings a metaphor creates is to relate two concepts in a new way. Then, to reverse the process, if we want to learn a new concept, we might do so by relying on the ferrying capacity of a metaphor. By bringing together two concepts already familiar (such as "marriage" and "zero-sum game"), we comprehend something unfamiliar. We work the implications back and forth until we are sure where the common features in the two events are, and where they are not. Einstein is reported to have said that space is curved, limited, and bounded. I am not sure that I understand the idea very well, but my understanding was improved by the metaphor that "space is a saddle—curved, limited, and bounded."

Learning also involves going from the familiar to the unfamiliar. We go from what we can claim correctly as familiar to the new meaning we wish to claim and to make our own. I. A. Richards thought that metaphors were "interactive" and "dynamic." In the sense that one part of the metaphor *tells on* the other part, I think I understand what Richards means. Something seems to happen to use when we first read a fresh metaphor. We reorganize our patterns of previously organized meaning. In that sense disciplined exploitation of metaphor is a form of conceptual learning. Put differently, if we want to learn new concepts, we should ask the teachers to compose them into metaphors for us. An apt metaphor is probably better than an arid and formally stated hypothesis in trying to find out about something that is unknown. It seems widely to be the case that the frontiers of scientific inquiry are more readily explained metaphorically than formally. The formal reconstructions come later. And so it may be with complex conceptual human learning: get thyself a metaphor to ride the unknown. All the rest is algebra.

Learning facts requires different moves. A student learning facts should be able to read the record and trace the document back through the techniques of record-making to the event recorded. In a sense, to say concepts are operationalized is to specify how records of events are made, plus the detection in the record of the regularities in the events. Facts, however, can also be singular. That parts of the record remain unique or singular is unfortunately true. Perhaps this singularity makes facts so hard to learn. Their very property as "recorded events" means a kind of definiteness, concreteness, specificity, complexity, reliability. Facts are used to generate meaning in the sense of "X stands for Y." Recorded event "X" is taken to stand for "Y"; X means Y; we see the meaningfulness of these facts as they connect one with another. We have begun to "conceive" the facts—that is, see their relation to something else as a regular pattern. Nevertheless, the fact, to help generate meaning, must retain its concreteness or "object-ness" in order to be part of a relation. Both the "X" and the "Y" in the formula for meaning must be capable of independent status in order to serve as the parts of the relation that are connected.

It also works the other way around: As concepts change, what is referred to in the recorded events may be different. The back-and-forthness between facts and concepts permits progress and continuity in a science. One need not be committed to either an inductionist or deductionist position in epistemology, taking as the key feature the decision about whether instances (facts) generate concepts (inductivist) or concepts generate instances (deductivist). Both views taken together seem inadequate to account for fact-making and concept formation. Again, the epistemological role of records of events is signally important.

Learning Methods

A method is a procedural commitment. We speak of the experimental method in science, and what we mean is a systematic way of choosing to do one thing and not to do another thing. Experimental method usually involves manipulating some variable, making something happen experimentally. Observational method relies on the event happening "naturally" without our interference or intervention. Experimental biology makes the assumption that killing an organism to study it does not get in the way of what you want to find out. In observational nature study the assumption is made that such manipulations do get in the way and contaminate the phenomena of interest. The difference between the two methods is one of a commitment about how one is to proceed.

Learning methods means learning ways of working such as these. It means to be able to go consistently through a series of steps or decisions about what to do. A method is like a set of directions. Learning a method is learning to follow directions in order to record an event. Actually making records of events are the techniques of work. Methods are more general than techniques; techniques are many times more numerous than methods. There must be hundreds of techniques used by those who follow only one method. Certainly it is true of the experimental method that it has spawned dozens of different techniques for making records of the experimental events.

Learning methods is not difficult; mastering techniques is. In both cases actual experiences in making events happen seems to be a good idea.

Learning and Governance

The social context of interactions of teachers, students, and curriculum requires governance. Learners, teachers, and the curriculum make specific and special claims, and when these conflict, some rational and humane way must be found to settle claims so that pedagogy goes forward. (The concept of governance is more fully explored below in Chapter 6. The role of the teacher as governor was discussed above in Chapter 3.) Is there a special role in governance for which students are responsible? Yes, and the key idea is the student's individual responsibility for his or her own learning. Although it may seem easy to say that students *have* responsibility, we need to see how they can *take* responsibility.

Responsibilities of all sorts can be thrust upon children. Sometimes they object, and a tension develops between teachers (and parents) and students. Claims are in conflict. The tension reduces when the child learns that accepting responsibilities actually results in greater power: the child learns that the responsible agent has more say in what is worth doing, more choices to honor, more freedom of action. And so it is with learning. When children learn that they are actually responsible for their own learning, they gain power over the conditions of their lives.

Along with this general sense of responsibility, there are specific responsibilities students have in an educative event. One of these responsibilities is to pay attention so meaning can be grasped, and shared. The student must give back to the teacher some idea of meanings grasped and significance felt. The student is testing meanings at this point as a prior condition for learning them. The student is also testing the teacher to find out if the teacher made a mistake. Both must work together to share meanings, for unless the student takes responsibility for sharing meaning, the teacher is disenfranchised and cannot teach. For the teacher to have the right to teach the student has the duty to share meaning. This reciprocity of rights and duties is part of the condition of governance in educating. The student's next steps in learning come after these other responsibilities have been fulfilled.

At this point the teacher, too, has a special responsibility. The teacher needs to have knowledge about knowledge, and knowledge about learning. The teacher is properly thought to have responsibility for the subject matter of the curriculum (the teacher should know algebra, or poetry, or auto mechanics). The teacher must also have knowledge about knowledge (the structure of knowledge arguments). But the special responsibility is for knowing what learning means, and what learning about learning means.

Returning to the learning V. This V gives us knowledge about learning. It shows us elements of knowledge in their relation to other elements. This knowledge now becomes directive in learning something new. If the point of the new learning is a new concept, then we know we should try to relate this new concept both up and down the structure of the V. We know we should try to relate the concept to events by searching for regularities in events to which the concepts refers. We know, further, we should relate the new concept to other concepts by searching for its place on a concept map, or its place within a conceptual structure. And so it would be with any new element to be learned. Find out what kind of epistemological element is it (a concept, a fact, a knowledge claim), see how that element functions in the knowledge structure, and take appropriate action after this analysis to fit the new to the old.

Knowing the structure of knowledge gives us knowledge about what to do in any new learning experience. We fit the new to the old as we see where it fits knowledge structure. Having knowledge about knowledge gives us a powerful way to regulate our learning about learning. Once we have learned about learning (Gregory Bateson calls this "deutero-learning" in *Mind and Nature* [1979], and thinks it is a function of evolution), we have second-order knowledge that can drive powerfully and efficiently our subsequent learning and the creation of first-order knowledge.

Learning and Teaching

Human beings learn many things. Among the most significant is learning about learning. This special knowledge of learning about learning is pointedly useful to the activities of teaching. Teachers should know their subject, and they should know about learning. Perhaps the key concept of these events is *reflexivity.* In taking the self as an object, we are providing a feedback loop to ourselves. It is as if we are doing one thing with two questions in mind: What am I doing, and what am I learning about what I am doing? If I am learning factoring in algebra, I am learning those concepts and skills; when I become reflexively aware of my learning, I am learning about my learning. In some ways these considerations are philosophic in nature. In philosophizing we make assertions, and then we ask questions about the assertions we just made (e.g., in probing undetected assumptions), and sometimes we extend it further and ask questions about our questioning. This moving up and down between levels of discourse greatly extends human intelligence. The heightened awareness that this reflexive thinking brings in the context of learning about learning is especially important to the teacher's knowledge about teaching.

Knowledge of these events can be obtained by every person who thinks about his own learning. And that, of course, includes teachers. Teachers learn many things. They can learn about learning by paying attention to their own instances of learning, and then reflecting on them. What teachers already know and value is what they should begin with in their analysis of their knowledge, and of their own learning (Fenstermacher 1979). Just as we begin with students in midstream—with that they know and claim to need to know—so too should it be with teachers. To get knowledge about learning to learn, begin with yourself. See what you know and value, and try to understand how you got that way. When you have learned to do this for yourself, then you can begin to help your students to do the same thing.

This self-awareness is often painful and difficult to achieve. One of the difficulties is the lack of good records of the events of self-awareness. Viewing videotapes of our teaching performance can provide us with records. We can study the facts. They are certain to evoke restlessness about ourselves. We do not immediately like what we see and feelings of distress get in the way of making sense of our actions. Yet when we persist in gaining self-knowledge, we can discharge our feelings and begin to think more clearly about the self as an object of knowledge. I am not recommending that we get bogged down with narcissism, self-listening, or self-aggrandisement. Self-awareness has pitfalls as well as promises. While we must learn as teachers to look at ourselves and not solely at students, what we find is not a general rule of learning for all students but only a rule for each of us to seek self-knowledge. The Socratic injunction to "Know thyself" can, as achieved, lead us to more caring and more knowledgeable teaching.

We should recognize that most human learning must be idiosyncratic, because each of us has undergone a life of learning unique to ourselves. Even though we seek to share meaning and to join in common purposes (we are social creatures), the vagaries of individual experience conduce to making learning an individual matter. In the best cases we see distinctive individuality. In ordinary cases suffused with blandness, some unique features will surely be found. Another point: teachers should not suppose that the way *they* learn is also the way their students will learn. Nevertheless, teachers can learn about learning by paying attention to their own learning as well as to that of their students.

This knowledge that teachers develop about their students is prepotent pedagogical knowledge. It will change with every class, every student, every subject matter. This knowledge makes teaching an art.

Educating is the context for our discussion of learning. We have not reviewed scientific studies of learning because they have failed us, and have done so because they so seldom have been placed in the context of educating. The search of science has been for laws and generalizations about learning that would fit into any time, place, and condition; the sorrowful fact is that no such laws have been formulated successfully. This chapter has presented a discussion of learning in the context of educating (as *one* of the four major interacting commonplaces). Should scientists care to reconsider their efforts to study learning, they would (or ought to) recognize that they cannot isolate learning from the other commonplaces if they wish claims about learning to have any effect in the context of educating.

In the context of educating, grasped meaning is what we learn. Activities of learning connect what we already know with the newly grasped meaning. The learner's knowledge powers learning: therefore, the most important thing about a learner is what that person can claim to know, and claim to need to know. As we become aware of what we already know through such devices as concept-mapping (a technique for externalizing our thinking), we become aware of the problem of learning: to connect the old with the new. Learning is the reorganization of meaning, and the old and the new must both be meaningful to the learner. The reorganization of meaning takes us several steps up from direct, immediate experience of the events of the world. We move from experiencing to grasping meaning to learning to knowing and finally to understanding. I have mapped these levels of learning on the Learning V. The Learning V is not a description of learning but is an heuristic device showing relations between knowing and learning. Epistemology, as a concern with the structure of knowledge, gives us a way to think about the structure of learning. I am not reducing epistemology to psychology, or knowing to learning. I am showing one way they might be related in the context of educating.

Meaning in the context of educating is always accompanied by feelings. Feelings are very important parts of the activities of learning—they work to combine the person-centered claims with the knowledge-centered claims. Grasped meanings when merged with feelings of significance create a powerful moment in educating.

Learners are viewed as the efficient cause of learning; therefore, they can be held responsible for learning. Responsible control over individual, idiosyncratic learning can be improved by considering concepts of studying. Studying is the task for which learning is the achievement.

CHAPTER SIX

Governance

Governance enters the context of educating because of the need to control the meaning that events are to have as educative events. Our main concern is with what we should think, feel, and do in order to control the meaning. Governance is power in a social setting which is required to bring together teaching, curriculum, and learning.

Governance concerns power. Through education we come into possession of our powers, and that includes power over educative events as well. When we consciously and deliberately make educative events happen, we have power over these events. But these events are social events, involving teachers and learners and other persons, and these events almost always involve a sharing of power. Teachers, typically, have power over students, but the curriculum has power over teachers. Students have power over their own learning if it is truly their *own* learning. The sharing of meaning between teachers and learners and curriculum requires the cooperation of all parties. Each of the three commonplaces must be harmonized if the educative event is to happen. The proper representation and protection of special claims and powers is the special power of governance, the fourth commonplace.

Governance is a special event of its own. We can develop concepts to use in thinking about its regularities. We come to see two events: a governing event as well as an educating event. Although they are often so intermixed that they appear to be the same thing, we can, through the use of appropriate concepts, see them as separate. Just as we have analyzed teaching, curriculum, and learning separately, so, too, can we analyze governance.

Let me begin by offering a simple formula. *Governance controls the meaning that controls the effort.* The governing events control the meaning that controls the effort put into teaching, into curriculum, into learning. The definitions in this book of these commonplaces tell what counts and what does not count as an instance of teaching, curriculum, and learning. If, for example, one accepts the view that teaching is the achievement of shared meaning, then that idea tells a teacher what certain actions mean as examples of teaching. The meaning controls the effort. Teachers and students must work together over the curriculum until congruence of meaning is achieved. If learners, as students, recognize the necessary role they must play in the sharing of meaning, then specific actions are guided by this idea. Students who realize "grasping meaning" and "getting the point" and "feeling the significance" in the sharing of meaning will act, as students, very differently from those who do not understand this view of what is involved in educating. A curriculum which reveals the structure of knowledge and especially the relevant criteria of excellence will make the specific meaning accessible to teachers and students and will thereby control their efforts. Each of the four commonplaces has a role in governing the others: none is totally overriding of the others; they must interact, for each has a quality required by the others.

An example. Spelling tests were given every Friday in my elementary school. A mark of 100 was perfect—twenty words all spelled correctly. I still have a warm feeling about those spelling tests and the string of 100's after my name. A grade of 90 or 95 or 100 meant an A; 80–90, B, 70–80, C, 60–70, D; and anything below 60 was F, failure. Some variation of this marking scheme was found in other areas of schooling. A 98 meant A+, but did it also mean that it was just two points shy of "perfect"? Did a 55 in art mean failure, gross imperfection? Could anyone score higher than 100? At Yale graduate school words replaced numbers. A "pass" was equivalent to the gentleman's "C," a high pass was, therefore, better, and "Honors" meant the highest grade, what an "A" or "100" stood for in other places of schooling. Clearly there is some justice and some arbitrariness in these marking schemes. As indicators of "success" or "progress," they carried very important *meanings.* A grade of 95 *means* an A to pupils in that system. By controlling grades, the effort of studying and learning can also be controlled.

Power over events comes from controlling meaning. We govern through mediated meanings. By telling ourselves and others what events mean, we come to make sense of our experience, and we come to have power over nature and experience. Meaning is social. When meanings are constructed so that we "get the point," that arouses our powers, animates our interests, and leads us on to new events. We see connections in events. Meanings are social constructions that enable us to exercise the powers of inference, of self-understanding, and of thoughtful action—all of which permit us to come to agreements, to share purposes, to control events in terms of what we think they should mean. Governance derives from shared meanings, some of which are taken as controlling.

Shared meaning is what makes educating possible (compare above, Chapter 2). Sharing meaning is also particularly important at the points of choice where activities of educating are governed. We have here one basic phenomenon working in two related but different ways. *The construction of meaning not only derives from the social setting, but also works to govern the social setting.* Devices of social control work on this principle. Social control is necessary in educating because educating is a social event. Social events are controlled by controlling the meaning they are to have. As we create meaning out of human experience, we create forms of permissible social interaction. In human history many such forms have been invented. Wars and other disputes of power have followed from the invention of different forms of social control. Fascism, socialism, democracy are names given to some of these inventions. The important point is to realize that these forms *are* social inventions; are social constructions; they exist as social realities. Our social constructions are not as obvious as skyscrapers, steel bridges, or federal highways, yet such physical constructions are created as a consequence of social constructions developed to give shape and meaning to human existence. Social constructions create meaning and permit us to do one thing and not another because of the meaning attributed to them.

This theory of educating focuses on changing the meaning of experience. But notice, not only does educating change the meaning of experience, but new meanings work to stabilize further changes in experience. Not only is learning the active reorganization of meaning, but reorganized and reconstructed meanings govern subsequent learning. Thus if we wish to govern educative events, we should look to what we need to think about and do to control the meaning educative events are to have.

Three sources of ideas help us here. The first one I have briefly discussed—namely, the social construction of meaning. This idea is fundamentally important to the process of educating and therefore is the aspect of governance most closely related to events of educating. The Governance V (Figure 5) will demonstrate the relationships between the three related sources and the governance event. This chapter will focus on the left side of the V first and then deal with the right side.

Governance whether of persons or procedures serves to make the claims of all contribute to the educative process. The most important thing about an educator as a governor is the way claims are validated. If the educative process would run its own course without guidance or governance, administrators would be out of a job. The educative process is not a natural process like the sun or the tides, which do not depend for their existence upon volitional agents. The educative process is artifactual and depends upon agents for its existence as well as its meaning. Although artifactual, the process has regularities; consequently, rational claims about the process can be warranted. We can recognize educating as a governed process some form of which is found in any culture that survives. In a progressive and democratic social order the overarching value of governance is social justice.

The most telling question for governance is this: How do we secure cooperation among people so that mutually shared purposes can be achieved? A second potent question is this: What concepts and procedures settle conflicting claims in the context of educating? The first question can be taken as assuming that power over others is derived from shared experience. The sec-

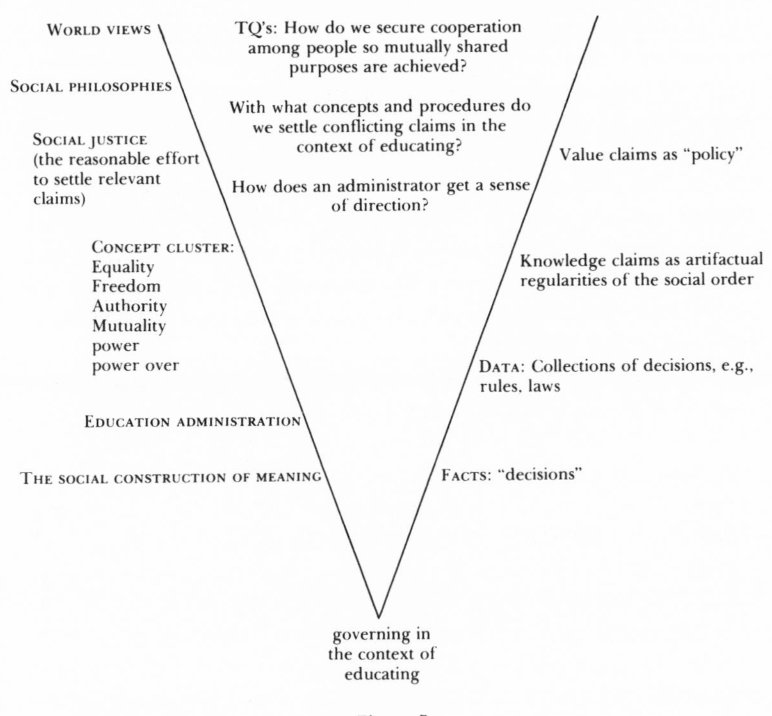

Figure 5.

ond question assumes that derived power can in turn be used to make decisions, to order claims, to direct further experience such that educative events will continue to take place. Educational administration is the reasonable effort to please everybody in the light of their legitimate claims for educating. This point assumes what in current practice is not very often the case—that administration in education should be concerned with educative events themselves. Other concerns should derive from this primary concern. But until we regain the notion that the chief purpose we have for schooling is educating, administrative practice will continue to mislead us.

A third telling question, getting us closer to the operations of administrative practice, is this: How does an administrator get a sense of direction? Put differently, how does an administrator know what he or she ought to do, ought to think, ought to feel? Granted that there is no set of rails underlying reality for us to put our trolley on; granted that there is no fixed star in the heavens on which to chart our course; granted that we are dealing with artifactual, not natural, regularities—the development of a sense of direction is nevertheless a most important task for administrators and administration. It is, moreover, a never-ending task, because the conditions and consequences of educating are open-ended, creative, inventive, changing because we are dealing with live creatures themselves in principle changing, and changed by the process of educating. The question of the proper process brings us back to the point of the V: the educating events and the governing events.

Let us now turn to the left side of the V and the related three sources of ideas. The social construction of meaning has already been discussed. A second source of relevant ideas comes from the theory and practice of administration. Educational administration is the name given in professional education to a specialization in certain forms of governance.

A Meaning Theory Approach to Educational Governance

Administrators must make decisions. They are daily confronted with issues. As Robert Frost wrote, "God is provident; he will supply the issues." Dispute and disagreement are part of the existential working conditions of an administrator.

Let us suppose the administrator is working with the board of education, seeking agreement on a basic educational issue. Agreement, this administrator believes, is a necessary condition for conjoint action. But agreement may be about a number of different things, based on different grounds and supported by different reasons. The Board and the administrator may agree to act in concert on one particular issue, such as policy on salary scales for teachers. Submerged in this agreement, however, may remain fundamental differences in value orientations. That is, they may agree or reach agreement for many different reasons: being lodge brothers; common concern for the welfare of teachers; because of competition with a neighboring community (pride in community); because of the dominant influences of status, persons, etc.; common perception of facts, of values, of psychosocial attitudes. On the other hand, they might simply agree to agree in order to act to observe the consequences of their decisions as providing tangible evidence of which point of view has greater empirical support.

Hence, agreement may be found at these points:

1. Conceptual meanings: theory, conceptual framework; e.g., "These ideas relate to these ideas."
2. Personal-social meanings: psychosocial customs; e.g., "We've always done it that way" or "Community X is doing it that way now."
3. Empirical meanings: the empirical facts as revealed by empirical inquiry within an agreed-upon frame of reference; e.g., "These concepts signify these regular events and records."

The Administrator as Executive

Agreement established at just one of these three places is inadequate and incomplete. Let us show how this might work.

If the agreement is a conceptual meaning, its form and argument might look something like the executive role of administration. Suppose we have an agreed-upon policy. For the administrator to make correct decisions (or to act properly), one need only study the statutes of policy and past decisions made in light of that policy. The duty of the administrator, then, is to accept the ethical content of the policy, not to question why. If the policy is wrong, the private citizen, through the elective process, will pass the ethical judgment and elect new board members. The social good is a collective pooling of private goods. Were administrators to intorduce personal values and definition of the good, they would be guilty of confusing private with public justice. The power of policy is the power of sovereign peoples whose bases for ethics are private and subjective. Except as a citizen, the administrator refuses to express the good. They seek agreement on what the policy is, and then proceed, dutifully, to implement it. The meaning of agreement is a conceptual meaning, leaving out empirical and psychosocial meanings. Such agreement is truncated and limited, but achievable.

As an example of this approach to administration, we may cite Woodrow Wilson (1887), who urged the adoption of "the lasting *maxims* of political wisdom" and "the permanent truths of political process." He recommended that the study of administration "secure executive methods from the confusion and costliness of empirical experiment and set them upon foundations laid deep in stable *principles*" (italics mine). These stable principles were for Wilson, as for many twentieth-century administrators, to be found in religion, in the cultural heritage of fixed ends and fixed means. The supreme end was freedom, the absolute means were such formal rules as parliamentary process, including majority vote and protection of minorities. The economic theory of Adam Smith went unquestioned.

The educational counterpart in administration was the school executive. Many of the first school superintendents were rugged individualists.

A Criticism of Individualism

School executives insofar as they are patterned after the style of nineteenth-century individualism most likely fail because of a faulty notion of the nature of society. The social order is something more than the accidents of individuals seeking their own personal goals. The old notion of one man's freedom ending at the point of another man's nose seems inadequate. People are interdependent in ways never dreamed by the ideology of individualism. Failing to understand the psychosocial cultural agreements of groups of people, school executives fail. (Like a general with a horse shot out from under him, the school executive has no support, no dynamic force to carry him.) The fact is that society changes, and this older pattern of thought, however good it was for an earlier time, is inadequate to newer social conditions.

Nevertheless, let us retain this one notion. It still remains important that the individual person—whether school executive or not, but especially the school executive—seek to understand and read one's own conscience. The executive must make clear to himself or herself the truths this person seeks to believe. Autonomy—if only over one's own decisions—is of great value. Autonomy and self-direction do not imply infallability. We may be cocksure of what we feel and believe, and still be wrong. But a sense of personal self-worth seems prior to a sense of self-direction. The chief value to be retained from individualism is the requirement that each person make up his or her own mind.

To be a mature, self-reliant, intelligent, and hard-working individual is an achievement; it is not a given; it is not a fixed condition of human nature. And while the processes of competition contribute to individuality, so may many other processes, such as aesthetic drive to pursue learning for its own intrinsic rewards (has nothing to do with how others in the race are doing). Competition against such things as disease, ignorance, and aggression may lead one into self-development just as well, and perhaps better than economic competition. It is still difficult, even for the most rugged individuals, to contemplate their own self-ruin with grace!

The Administrator as Group Process Leader

As the social order changed, reaction against the individualistic school executive developed. A new approach to administration was worked out, seeking leadership by the people. It carried many labels: democratic administration, group-centered leadership, human relations in administration. Each of these labels indicates the basic assumption that, as Carl Sandburg wrote, "Everybody knows better than anybody." A broad base for decision ensures that leadership will be not autocratic but democratic. Common problems are faced together, and the desire to achieve a solution that will not trample on anyone's toes ensures effectiveness. Decisions may take longer to reach in this model, but there will be less backtracking afterward. The basis of the good becomes what everyone can agree on, and consensus of belief becomes the definition of truth. Responsibility is fixed, since decisions made by the group are enforced by the group, for the good reason that those who are affected are those who participated in making the decision.

It should be apparent that this form of argument concerning agreement is based upon personal-social meanings. This notion of agreement cannot be understood apart from personal-social-cultural *de facto* norms. People may agree to the policy propositions, but what will they actually live up to in association with one another? The basis of their agreement is that they know what "his folks will do and won't do no matter what." The Eighteenth Amendment, prohibiting alcoholic beverages, carried all the power of high policy, but its conceptual-policy meaning was violated every day by the psychosocial meanings that dominated living with one's fellow humans.

Social scientists, studying groups of people, refer to *patterns* of culture—not collections of atomistic individuals, but coherent patterns. Values are intimately involved in these patterns, which in turn seem to determine the effectiveness of high policy. The people *do* what feels right whether or not they know what is right. Policy, then, gains its standards for judging its worth or effectiveness from the patterns of behavior of social groups. The wise administrators, then, first find out what their constituents will put up with, and construct policy accordingly. But their policy is not hortatory or merely subjective, but empirically testable against the group with which they work. Such policy tends to perpetuate itself, based upon residues deposited from past experience. Policy is, therefore, more or less static, while social agreements change. Policy, therefore, tends to become bad and in need of reform in the light of the patterning of actual social agreements. Administrators who have seen their community change rapidly from semirural to suburban can feel the conflict generated by shifts in the meaning of agreements regarding school policies. The "good" can be derived (not deduced) from the "is" if the special context (or local ecology) is specified. Standards for judging the "ought" can be derived from the "is" if the "ought" is one thing (e.g., policy) and the "is" another (e.g., personal-social-cultural agreement).

The administrator who has had the opportunity to move from one position to another will recognize that the personal-social-cultural agreements of the former community may not be found in the new community. As a consequence, policies that were effective in the former situation may be radically ineffective in the new situation. We may conclude that subcultures exhibit ethical heterogeneity and pluralism. Uniform policy fails, therefore, to correspond adequately to changing and pluralistic social agreements. *Merely* psychosocial agreement is inadequate because of the confusion between group process and empirical inquiry. A consensus of feelings may tell us nothing about empirical conditions. Empirical inquiry must be instituted for such knowledge. Wishing never made it so, for an individual or for a group of individuals pooling their wishes. When group process has resulted merely in emotional catharsis—not leading to a quest for a rational principle or empirical inquiry—the work of the world has seldom got done, even though everyone for a while has felt good about it.

Not all group process is bad. The point is that some group process that sought consensus, with the presumption that it (*consensus gentium*) established truth, had the effect of stopping inquiry. Moreover, it is likely that administrators felt guilty about its ineffectiveness but even more guilty when, out of good conscience and a concern to get on with the affairs of the schools, they resorted to covert manipulation of the group. Without clear statements of democratic principles or goals, the supposedly democratic means of group process can easily be used to reach nondemocratic ends. Group process, taken as means alone, can work toward any end, but it is fallacious to assume that because the means are democratic means, *any* ends thereby established will be democratic ends.

The Administrator as Social Scientist

Moving from the individualist, with the concern for principle and from the human relations expert with concern for people in groups, we find another development in administration: the recent interest in treating administration as a social science. Many research efforts during the past fifteen years have taken the behavioral science approach to the study of educational administration. One of the assumptions often made is that the study of administration is the same no matter what organization is being governed. Thus it does not matter whether one studies church administration, school administration, business administration, or military administration, because all have in common administrative functions in complex social institutions. The study of administration is the study of that phenomenon, no matter where it happens to take place. Imagine a large diagram with encompassing lines drawn around Administration and smaller circles showing "education" or "business" subordinate to administration. Some researchers assert a variety of claims about organization and administration which are not specific to one institution. Such assertions indicate administrative functions of recruitment of personnel, allocation of resources, system maintenance, system expansion, inputs and outputs, efficiency, and so on. One way to view these assertions is as the analysis of the idea of "system" itself. Anything called a system has parts, has exchange within and between systems, has functions, has size (which can vary), takes up space, and needs energy or resources to sustain it. These assertions are true by virtue of the meaning of the concept "system." No empirical studies are needed (Green 1980).

When one begins to find empirical referents for these logical claims, the nature of the assertions changes because the conceived regularities are different. And the starting-point assumption also changes, because a prior assumption now has to be made explicit. One now has to make clear what counts as an instance of "educational organization" or "business organization." Is New York University, for example, an educational or business organization? Or both—namely, a good example of bad business administration at places where it is a good example of educational administration? The Catholic Church system has been described as an excellent example of efficient administration even though the logical doctrines vary from country to country and even *because* of the catholicity of doctrines embraced. To take one more confounding instance: is a navy hospital an example of military or hospital administration? These perhaps specious examples boggle the mind only when one fails to see that administration is studied as means-centered phenomena and it is assumed that different ends make no difference to the actual means used. The science of administration abstracts itself into logical networks of possible relations, makes assertions that appear to be empirical but often can be reduced to an elaboration of meaning of the key terms. One need not be put off by refinement of concepts; but one must always ask for a specification of the eventful regularities to which the concepts refer. If they refer only to other concepts, then we know we must continue the analysis until at some point we touch ground. One assumption of this book aimed at grounding claims is that the specification of what is and is not *educational* is an analysis that comes before any assertions about what is and is not *administration*. Partly for this reason we have used the terminology "Educational governance" in place of "educational administration."

The science of administration has theories that purport to account for all relevant facts. The kind of agreement established here is an agreement between theory and facts, between the conceptual dimension of meaning and the events and objects or empirical dimension of meaning. How can the administrator gain a sense of direction from scientific theory? Since it is widely held that science deals with facts and excludes values, how is the good to be determined? How can one find out what one "ought" to do?

With some scientists, it is thought that nature supplies empirical meanings. The events and things of direct experience are used to validate the three categories of meaning. Scientifically verified *theory* (tested against the "is" of empirical meanings) may provide a cognitive standard against which to judge conceptual meanings, and these in turn serve as a standard against which to judge concept-principle-theory meanings.

Concretely, this means that a person confronted with the flux of experience selects some empirical meanings as key facts. These key facts are the basis for defining, remembering, ordering, and anticipating all other meanings. To discover what the key facts or meanings are in any given culture or subculture is to discover the basis for making value judgments. Theories containing these facts may be in error. I quote Northrup (1957: 449):

> Consequently, human behavior which is in part at least the consequence of primitive assumptions concerning first order facts qua theory may be in error also. No philosophy, from which we derive ethics, ever captured a vast body of people unless it seemed to be required by specific first order facts in their experience.
>
> "Good" is the name for the empirically verifiable theory of first order facts when this theory is taken as the theoretical standpoint for guiding human behavior and evaluating its artifacts . . .
>
> "Ought" is the for-me-ness of such theory. The making of a true theory mine occurs when, by appeal to (a) first order facts which are (b) mine, I find the (c) theory to be empirically verified by or for me.

Just how scientific theory in administration is to supply administrators with guides to action is not entirely clear. It should be clear, however, that the bases for moral behavior will need to be worked out carefully. Some social scientists wish to make a radical break between facts and values, between the "is" and the "ought." It is up to them to tell us how they are to be related, supposing the radical break to be a valid one. This much I think I see: if one is to approach administration from a theory of meaning, the complete conception of meaning is needed. One needs to discover the key empirical meanings that support the theoretical meanings. And the psychosocial artifactual meanings will have to be tied to facts and theories. I think that it is possible to find support from this three-legged stool, the meaning triad. At any given point of analysis, each dimension may be examined while the others are held constant. Analysis leading to vision and understanding seems to require some ground to stand on which is not being analyzed at the time. We may work out theory *qua* theory, or theory and facts, while holding psychosocial artifactual meanings constant (which is a meaning of objectivity). But at some point the psychosocial artifactual meanings will need to be examined, and both theory and fact will be held constant (which is a meaning of relevance). Let me try to make these abstract statements clearer by reference to role theory in administration. *The distinction between the "is" and the "ought" is both illuminating and misleading.*

Is theory a guide to action? The relation between theory and action is similar to the relation between thought and action. Role theory is a theory of action; there should be no problem about its relevance to action. As a theory of action, it assumes action already occurring. It assumes that there is a social system operating. It assumes that goals have previously been selected, defended, and projected. Goals are operative. Nevertheless, there does remain a concern in that it does not tell administrators how to act. They feel they must still use their common sense, their judgment, the qualities that made them leaders in the first place, including artfulness and finesse. The scientists reinforce this conviction by asserting that a theory—as an abstract set of relations analogous to a map—contains no "ought" judgments. It is a map, not an actual journey; it can be a guide for the journey, but it can never tell one to travel, nor, especially, can it tell them where they ought to go.

This line of argument does seem to build confusions rather than eradicate them. One administrator claims that he makes no decision without consulting role theory. He testifies that he constantly refers to the map before charting his course. The theory may be wrong, but it serves as a screen, a way of thinking about his administrative behavior. Used in this way, the role theory turns out to be not a theory of action so much as a theory of *thought*. The theory has its relevance as a precursor to action as a *way of thinking* about what actions to take. The theory turns out to be a set of related concepts, and we use concepts in thinking.

The theorists or social scientists tell us that the theory contains no "ought"; it will not tell us what to do. But do they tell us that the theory contains no "is's" either? A map contains no rocky hills, no noisy brooks, no hot sands. Maps contain conceptual relations, not empirical or psychosocial relations. Maps, or scientific theories, are supposed to function to establish relations among "is's," and typically they do this relating by some principle of correlation, correspondence. A major difficulty arises when things are themselves abstractions and seldom directly point-at-able. The philosophic error is that naming implies existence. Where is a person's "personality"? Where is the "role conflict"? Where is "a goal," "a social system"? Indeed, after the line of "this will be good for the institution" where *is* an institution? The role theory map is a map among these things: social systems, institutions, roles, expectations, goals, personalities and so on. But these things are themselves only names: they may be reduced to things or events through operational definitions, or denotations, but the theory does not do this reduction; hence, we can conclude again that the theory contains no "is's," and refers to "is's" and their relations from a great distance of abstraction. It is little wonder that some administrators have difficulty using the theory as a guide to action.

Moreover, the theory does contain, by direct implication, some "oughts." These "oughts" to be sure are conditional oughts, not unconditional or absolute oughts. As Northrup suggests, "ought" is the for-me-ness of theory. For example, one may infer that if you want to use the role theory, and you do want to, then, you ought to use it correctly. That is, you are not permitted by the rules of the theory to import a Skinnerian or S-R explanation of the ways conflicts are resolved. Nor could you convert a nomothetic principle into a nomological principle and still retain the original model.

A carpenter's manual is a guide to action. A musical score is a guide to action. Monographs on surgery contain guides to operations. The alphabetical tabs of an indexed dictionary are a shortcut guide to finding words beginning with the same letter. A code of ethics is a guide to action (e.g., NEA codes for teachers, AMA codes for doctors). The sign "In case of fire break glass, reach inside, open door, exit on fire escape at rear" is a guide to action. These guides contain conditional oughts. They seem to proclaim: if you want such and such result, then act this way. If you want to use the fire escape, then you ought to break the glass. If you want to build a garage as a do-it-yourself project, then you ought to do it the way the blueprint says. These are conditional oughts, not absolute oughts, but they carry some of the meaning of ought nevertheless.

After saying that there is a sense in which you ought to use the theory in its own terms—theories *qua* maps do not contain either "is" or "ought"—let us reverse the analysis: A map contains both "is's" and "oughts." The empirical data which make the abstract *relations* relevant may be established. The *relations* constitute the "is's." The relation between river and town *is*. The rules or directions on how to use the map (for one mile read one inch, etc.) *ought* to be followed. If you want to use the map to get some place, then you ought to use it correctly. The data made relevant by experimental inquiry which tends to support the theory constitute the key facts. The directions for the use of the instrument (the theory) constitute the relevant "oughts." But we can have neither an "is" nor an "ought" without stipulating a third element: the context, which must include the agent or operator. In other words, to clarify meanings, we must specify the three components of a theory of meaning: conceptual, psychosocial, empirical. The formula "A is a sign of C to B" must be filled out with referents. Role theory formation (sign-sign) is a sign of relations (persons and things) to the administrator (agent).

A map has reference if one uses inference. But a map has

reference to an "is" (terrain) only if some action is performed by some human agent. Some context for so behaving is necessary. Furthermore, a map has reference to an "ought" (a goal) only if some act of thought is performed by some human agent, the for-me-ness judgment. The context or frame of reference, including the agent or person using the map as well as the thing or event referred to by the map, must be included for an analysis of the meaning of the theory.

Finally, let me suggest a metaphor by which to interpret the theory of meaning. I shall call it the leaky pail theory of meanings—a name that is a variant of Popper's statement that Plato had a bucket theory of mind. The leaky pail theory is a way to give meanings containment, for a time, but not ultimate containment. It gives meanings shape but only for a time because experience changes, people change, things change, ideas change. The leaky pail gives us no more than a way to hold the stuff for a while.

Recent work in educational administration has been stimulated by conceiving of administration as a science, and research and recommendations in administration derive largely from scientific knowledge. The scientific paradigm accepted in administration is curiously sterile. Professionals in administration are at a low point of credibility. Whether this disenchantment is a consequence of a sterile and limited view of science or from some other cause, the probability is high that further persistence along those lines is unlikely to provide us with what we need in educating.

Perhaps foremost in importance, because it has often been neglected as a specific study, is the concern that administrators must be able to deal with concepts. They must learn to deal with concepts directly if they are to improve their thinking. Facts and data will never carry the day, for without appropriate conceptualizations facts are blind. There is nothing inscribed on the face of a fact that tells us how to think about it; for that we need concepts. I dare say that more improvement in administrative practice would come from systematic focus on the conceptual side of knowledge than through any other single approach. But in addition, and this view is certainly not popular, the domains of knowledge most relevant to administration are ethics and social philosophy. So uncritically held is the assumption that scientific knowledge exhausts all of knowledge that philosophical knowledge is not even thought of as knowledge. Knowledge about what constitutes social justice is supremely important knowledge for administrators. Knowledge about the conceptual distinctions surrounding the concept of equality is likewise important. Knowledge about educating found in philosophies and theories of educating surely is indispensable for anyone who would act responsibly in the context of educating. These sources of knowledge need to be made accessible to administrators-in-training if they are to help get educating under intelligent control.

In American society the concept of equality is widely accepted as desirable. Equality of opportunity is typically regarded as a question of priority of social values. For our purposes it is important to see equality as a concept. As a concept it is ambiguous and therefore requires conceptual analysis.

Equality: The Primary Idea

Of all the key concepts of governance, equality is the primary one. It is primary in two ways: as the first idea which needs consideration, and as the basic idea on which others build. If conditions of equality can be established in fact, then progress toward mutuality can be expected. A fairly detailed analysis, both logical and analogical, is presented here in the attempt to show how basic the equality concept can be.

Preliminary Distinctions. Three aspects of the concept must be distinguished. In ordinary language, equality as a concept is expressed as (a) a value claim, (b) as a factual claim, and (c) as a conceptual claim. In the logical analysis that follows we are concerned with conceptual claims. These conceptual claims we divide into two definitional forms, the extensional and the intensional. Extensional definitions of equality typically make equality a term indicating a relation. Hence, we speak of equality *of* something: opportunities, treatments, outcomes, benefits. (Much of the social distress surrounding the notion of equality is the slippage in meaning from equality of opportunities to equality of benefits. It is as if we failed to realize that opportunities for something do not guarantee that we will receive that something.) In the substantive analysis that follows, I claim that as we shift from opportunity to treatment to benefit, the basic meaning of equality shifts from sameness to fairness to uniqueness. In the progressive realization of equality we find equality changing from same opportunity (the door of education is open to all), to fair treatment (we can treat people differently and still treat them fairly), to unique benefit (wide diversity of outcome is to be expected and prized).

Logical Analysis of the Concept of Equality

Several subconcepts are relevant: uniqueness, identity, equivalence, sameness, and fairness.

Uniqueness or Identity. The discipline of mathematics makes a distinction between the concepts of "equal" and "equivalence." The concept of equal can be explained in the language of set theory. Of any two sets, A and B, if A is a subset of B and B is a subset of A, then we can write the equal sign between them as "A equals B." This sense of equal means that all the elements in A are the *same* as all the elements in B. They are the identical elements. Thus the meaning of A equals B is that A is just another way to write B; A is the name of B in different words; there is no difference between A and B because A is identical to B. Thus A is *nothing but* B.

To speak of "an equal" is to refer to an existent, or entity, not a relation. To speak of "equality" is to refer to a relation between entities. As an expression of a relation, equality is "of" something. So we speak of equality *of* opportunities, equality *of* treatment, equality *of* benefits.

When we speak of individuals as equals we are according them status as entities and not initially comparing them. We do not compare them to one another or to any standard of judgment which describes in what respects they are equal. We are naming them as unique persons, and that is all. We claim that persons are of equal worth and that they are incomparable. We do not have to assume an "essence" of persons which all persons have (as a common humanity) which *makes* them equals. We do not have to pull back the veil to see their soul, or their rational faculties, or their pineal gland. We might want to see if they had use of a language. But even there we do not need to decide that "essential language-bearing quality" is what makes them equal. We are concerned with what makes them persons in a social sense—namely, that they can communiate with others and with themselves. A person in the company of peers is coexistent with equals, with entities that have existence as persons. Any further analysis reveals their *distinctiveness* as unique individuals, or commonalities shared with others. But an "equal" in the sense of "men and women are equals" signifies the existence of an entity, a unique person.

This move in mathematical reasoning in the moral context pays off in a number of problematic situations. It is a technique of work to see if what some part of the problem called an A is the same as another part of the problem called a B. The reasoning rips off the disguise. The initial problem may suggest that A and B are different and the proof works to show they are the same, therefore cannot be different, and wherever before one wrote an A one can now write B as a correct substitute. The meaning of equality is *identity.* There is no equation between A and B because there is only a unique thing disguised as if it were two things. Mathematical generalization is achieved by the process of reduction of what appear to be different things to only one thing; we can then say more with a lot less, and generalization emerges.

Equivalence. The notion of equivalence is used when one wants to preserve differences in some respects between two things and to identify the similarity between them. Equivalence is a sign that two things are alike in some respects but un-alike (unlike) in other respects. For example, to say of two basketball teams that they have an equal number of players, namely five, is to say they are equal with respect to at least one feature, and equivalent in other features. Further, it suggests that the teams *will be* different with respect to other features. The mathematical sign $\cong$ is the sign for equivalence.

Sameness. In the meaning of equality as "sameness," we very nearly reach an arithmetical meaning. To say of two things that they are equal, say "$5 = 5$," for example, suggests that five basketball players on one team equals five on the other team, and that means they both have an equal number of players, a full team. The teams are equal in the number of players even though as they play the game it will be seen that individual players come and go and the uneven score at the end of the game will mean one team is unequal to the other in the game played. We must be careful not to make a mistake of supposing that "sameness" means "identity." If I say that in the expression "5 = 5" the term '5' is the same term as '5' *and as a matter of fact it is the identical number,* I would be making a mistake. It would be like saying "The term '5' is *nothing but* the term '5'. I would have committed the fallacy of reductionism; I would have rubbed out one element in the equation by reducing it to the other element. I would not have an equation. In order to say that "5 = 5" it must be the case that 5X is equal to 5Y if 5X and 5Y are exactly alike but not identical. When we put in the algebraic ciphers X and Y to stand for teams X and Y, we can see the abstract point.

Does 2 = 2? Where units are equal, the expression of the form of the *relation* is either the word "equal" or the sign " = ". The relation is one of indicating sameness but not identity. The terms in the equation can be related as equal only if the terms are exactly alike but not identical. The X is not reduced to the Y; the X is not (nothing but) the Y; the '2' is the same as the '2' and both 2's must have separate identities in order to be separate members of the equation. When we come to the moral judgment "Equals equal equals" we see the necessity of avoiding reductionism. If we say it is fair to "treat equals equally" we are saying "Treat X" and "Treat Y" such that X is equal to Y and the treatment given each is the same but not identical treatment. To say that persons are entitled to "equal pay for equal work" is not to say that the work they must do is the *identical* work. Neither arithmetically, nor practically it is possible for the work to be the identical work. A thing is what it is and not another thing; a thing must have its self-identity in order for it to become an item in an equation. Or for it to be a value in a variable. Moral equality presupposes separate identities of persons such that they can be members in the relation of equality. Practically it means that individuals express distinctiveness, uniqueness. To learn to prize such individuality in the best terms is a most sophisticated development of moral action. It is an *achievement* of human experience, not a given.

This piece of abstract reasoning is not, I hope, specious. We must carefully locate and distinguish the three elements needed to establish the statements we want to make about equality. One element is the *agent.* A second element is also an *agent.* And the third element is the expression of whatever it is that *relates* them. In the statement "X equals Y" we see the three elements: X, Y, and equals. In the statements "Equals equal equals" we see the same word standing for three referents, the X, the Y, and the relation between them. When we make the moral judgment "Treat equals equally," we also have three referents: "equal X" and "equal Y" and the "equal treatment." It is possible for us to give each equal the same treatment but not the identical treatment. We can, for example, teach both X and Y the same genetics but it will not be the "identical" genetics nor will the teaching be the "identical" teaching.

Fairness. The notion of fairness in arguments about social justice involves the assertion that it is fair to treat two equal (unique) persons differently if the standard for judging and applying such treatments is the same standard for both persons. For example, it is fair to spend more time with some pupils than with others if the others are also being given the same educational treatment—namely, the education they can make good use of or that is appropriate to their needs, abilities, and educational progress. The actual treatment of a slow versus a bright pupil may be different, but both are getting a fair shake because they are getting the best education they can use. Equality of educational opportunity would not fair if it were identical treatment (which it could not be, since we are talking about at least two individuals) or the same treatment as the same amount of education for the same amount of pupil work.

What does fairness mean? As a concept that children use all the time, it seems to be both a negative plea, "Don't step on me," and a positive proposition, "Let's make up a rule." One of the most successful of such rules is exemplified in the classic problem of "How big a piece is mine?" The rule is to let one person cut the cake or make size allotments, and for the next person to have first choice of a piece. This rule is fair because the making of the standard of judgment is jointly agreed to first, the use of the standard does not entail power over choices, and choices are voluntary and free from power constraints. And—it works! Not only to divide a cake or pie or piece of candy, but to set a standard for rules. It is a generative rule, a master rule in the sense of a master key of rules. And it works to satisfy choices made on grounds that are not always self-serving. A child may cut the pieces to be of different sizes knowing he or she may get the smaller; the other child *may* choose the smaller if not coerced into it, and the first child gets the larger piece of cake. The rule permits continuity and variation; once understood, it is often used, and the role changes are directly experienced by children. It is in capsule a lived occasion for the exchange of power roles, of leaders becoming followers, and the also-ran getting a chance to see how it feels to be in charge.

What does fairness mean? An experience of rule-governed distribution of the goods of life such that the experience can be repeated with continuing satisfaction with the governance of the rule. That is fair, is it not? The claims of all appropriately considered is the rule; the rule itself is subject to amendment. Conflicting claims are validated, and the outcome is mutual accommodation. Any rule that governs claims is a concept. A rule is a conception, but not all concepts are rules. A rule makes events have a pattern that agents share, hence rules (like concepts) point out commonalities in events. But a lot of concepts that function this way are not rules governing agents. The key concepts that shape major knowledge claims signify regularities in events which do not depend for their existence on volitional agents.

Equality: Three Analogies

In a brief space the use of common-sense analogies may be helpful in identifying a family of different meanings gathering around the concept "equality."

The Contest Analogy. The contest analogy draws attention to competition, to games and rules. As in a foot race, equal starting points and times for all contestants help to determine what the inequalities will be. Some individuals will run faster than others; inequality of outcomes is expected. Thus in educational practice children start school together at a given time of the year and are expected to run the same course following the same curriculum. Achievements at the end of the educational episode are expected to vary; approximately one third will do well, one third poorly, and the middle third will remain undistinguished. The mode of testing for achievement usually relies on some measure of equal units. The total number of problems solved or words spelled in a fixed amount of time is the yardstick often used. In this analogy equality is based on some concept of sameness. The same measure, the same unit, the same time, the same treatment. In part, the historic separate-but-equal doctrine was based on the claim that equal or same facilities imply equal opportunities to learn. This notion was struck down by the Supreme Court on the grounds that separate but equal facilities were inherently unequal. The same psychosocial conditions cannot exist for blacks and whites when they are separated into different schools. The reason often given for integration of schools as implying equality of educational opportunity is also based on a concept of sameness; the same psychosocial conditions.

The Hospital Analogy. Merely being together in a physical sense, however, does not in every case generate the same psychosocial conditions. There are inequalities and handicaps to learning which need to be compensated for. Some children, of all kinds, learn quickly and well; some learn slowly and poorly. Educational practices compensate for inequalities in the way that hospital treatment repairs deficiencies; the goal is genuinely equal treatment of all individuals. Here equality implies fairness. Fairness suggests that a pupil will not be asked to do what he cannot be expected to do, and that he will get help in doing what he can learn. We would not expect a boy with enthusiasm for baseball to become a Jimmy Pearsall or a Jackie Robinson, but we can expect to help him do better in the kind of game he can play. Compensatory education is fair even if achievements (outcomes) are disparate. It is fair that all pupils must learn to read and write (etc.), but not all need to finish at the same point of achievement. For some children actual achievement will be vastly superior to that of other children; they will solve more problems or read more books or extend themselves further in all directions if instruction is geared to their pace. A consequence of this notion of equal treatment is that facilities or resources may be provided unequally. Hence, we get a reversal of the first position: equal facilities do not imply equal opportunity to learn. Facilities must be differentiated for a continual opportunity to learn to be possible. Educational testing, under this analogy, is done by comparing individuals with their own starting point, not by comparing individuals to one another on some measure of equal units. In the hospital all in need are given differentiated treatment, but all are not expected to have the same quality of health or live to the same age. Some minimum of treatment is needed for all before they can be released from the hospital, or the educational task. In both cases the quality of improvement from the original state is seen as the basis of judgment. Comparison is from individual beginnings to an end, not from a fixed and common starting time to finishing time.

The Feast Analogy. From the somberness of the hospital analogy we move to the joyousness of the feast or festival analogy. Everyone invited to the feast is invited as an equal. Each person is expected to find his own joy, to do his own thing. No attempt is made to formalize competition or to treat for alleged deficiencies. Equality implies individuality, uniqueness, distinctiveness. Comparisons between persons are not made, because persons are of unique worth, incomparable. Equal opportunity implies a chance for social interactions not had before. Education, or festivity, is a function of many things: interests, talents, past experiences, desires, anticipations, the social stimulus engendered by other persons. Facilities are provided on the basis of the person's ability to make good use of them. Competence and interest are important factors in the actual distribution of goods. On this analogy a pupil would be tested only if he requested a test for his own guidance just as a person might wish to be checked out for his dancing skills before undertaking a new dance step. Pupils test themselves against the kinds of experiences they have undergone as a basis for anticipating new experiences. They see for themselves if they are equal to the task they desire. Just as festivals are occasions for the social community to provide for the joy of new experience, so should education be.

Analogies do not run on all fours. To the competitive, and much of America today remains extremely success-oriented, the meaning of sameness and the analogy of equality of runners in a race will appeal. To the healers the meaning of fairness and equality of differentiated treatment will appeal. To the value-seekers the meaning of uniqueness and the analogy of the festival will appeal. We have spent this much effort to clarify the notion of equality because in some sense it is the operating concept in educational governance. Governance should have enough power to *make* equality a state of affairs. Two other key concepts, freedom and authority, are also operating concepts, but they seem to work best in the context of previously established equality. See Table 1 for an analysis of equality.

Considerable space has been given to the definitions of equality. A distinction between intensional and extensional definitions is marked by the concepts of "equality" and "equality of." Inspect Figure 6. Here the three concepts of equality (sameness, fairness, uniqueness) are put into a matrix with the three concepts of equality of (opportunity, treatment, benefit). I have drawn arrows to indicate my preference for the relations between these ideas.

I think that equality of educational opportunity requires that each person be seen as the same as every other person. We all should have equal access to the chance for an education. Barriers to equality—whether elitism, social class distinctions, religious beliefs, sexual preferences, power of money—which close the door to opportunity are, in the long run, self-destructive because they cannot survive in an island of privilege in an ocean of ignorance. The educational door must be open to all.

Once the process of educating begins, however, equality becomes fairness, and differentiated treatment of indiviuals is required for the educative process to work. Educating will always result in differentiation. No matter how much alike individuals are at the beginning, the process of educating will have the effect of making them much more different at the end. Homogenized groups quickly become heterogenous. Meanings multiply through educating.

Table 1. Application of the conceptual meanings of equality to educational research, policy and practice

	Sameness	*Fairness*	*Uniqueness*
1. Opportunity	Same number of years of education required of all as minimum.	If pupil A is better than pupil B in any or all subjects, it is fair that he be given a higher grade or more years of education.	Equal opportunity implies a chance for social interaction not had before. Amount of education a function of other things: talents, interests, etc.
2. Finance	Average daily attendance basis for making dollar support equal.	If community A is poorer than community B, it is fair that it receive more dollars of support from state and federal sources.	Dollar support also given as a consequence of other factors: special interest, exceptional cases, new opportunities, one-in-a-lifetime events, novel proposals, unusual subjects.
3. Facilities	Equal facilities imply equal opportunity to learn.	Equal facilities do not imply equal opportunity to learn; facilities may be provided unequally in terms of some standard.	Facilities provided on the basis of the person's abilities to make good use of them; competence and interest factors.
4. Analogy	Contest analogy: equal starting points for all helps to determine what the inequities are but unequal outcomes, achievements are expected.	Hospital analogy: all treated, but some may die. Unequal treatment equalizes handicaps of birth; compensatory education is fair even if achievements are differentiated.	Open banquet analogy: education selected in terms of interests, desires, talents, skills.
5. Testing	Testing based on some fixed unit; e.g. number of problems solved in a fixed period of time.	Testing done by comparing improvement of the individual from his own starting point. Learning for mastery independently of the time taken.	Testing done only as requested by pupil for guidance; wider "testing" of social interaction used as pupils "test" themselves against experience undergone.

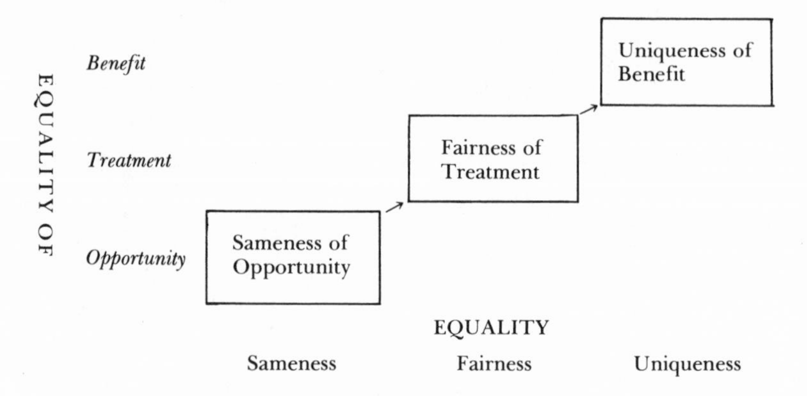

Figure 6. Equality as sameness of opportunity, fairness of treatment, and uniqueness of benefits as appropriate for different places in the educative process

As the process comes to its endings, the benefits of educating call attention to the uniqueness of achievement. Learning is idiosyncratic. Diversity is prized more than uniformity. Educational goods are distributed through individuals, not through aggregation. As equality in all the senses described above is achieved, the concepts of freedom, authority, and mutuality become of greater concern.

The concept of equality, especially relevant to governance, has been analyzed in detail. The remaining three concepts will be briefly examined.

Freedom

Freedom enters the educative process at many places. At the place where we are concerned with the authority of the role of the teacher, the freedom to become an authority must be supported—that is, a version of academic freedom is called for. The teacher who is to become an authority must have *freedom for* learning. There must be command of the concepts and methods of an area of study; the teacher must have the power to command knowledge in an area. Usually we think a college education is sufficient for this level of knowledge, but often in practice we find college graduates who do not know the structure of knowledge of their academic major. They have not been taught it because their professors did not teach it (whether *they* even knew it may be in question). The educational governor must be concerned with this problem—the problem of the claim to expertise.

In addition to the power to learn, the freedom *for,* there must be a freedom *from.* This freedom is from the vicious interference of vested interests which do not want truth but want to protect their interests by any means other than legitimate inquiry. Where the issues are hot issues, the need for disciplined and slow and regular truth-seeking increases. Confronting issues fairly takes much practice. Confronting issues to protect the legitimate claims of properly interested parties is a complex skill needed by educational administrators. Methods and procedures for adjudicating claims are the special knowledge of educational governance. When it comes to teacher claims, the potent concepts of authority and freedom must be clearly understood.

Authority

An authority is a person who makes or creates something, as an author who writes a book. The terms "authority" and "author" come from the same root, *auctor.* It is easy to see that in common usage there has been an erosion of the meaning of authority from the person who is the source of power—author—to the person who exercises power. Authority now means the right to give commands and enforce obedience. In the worst sense, it is authoritarianism, the power to coerce unquestioning obedience, including death of the disobedient. The problem arises when the source of power is disconnected from the use of power. In all cases where authority is exercised, we should be able to question the claim of authority, to go back to the author and see what right the author has to command our attention.

Ascribed authority is power given to a person; achieved authority is a power earned by that person. Unfortunately, to become a teacher or a parent in this society carries with it much more ascribed authority than achieved authority. Most parents do not have much sensible self-achieved knowledge of rearing children. They could be thus educated, but most are not. Yet in many states the ultimate authority, or ultimate responsibility, for the education of children resides in the parent. The rule "in loco parentis" is a way of recognizing that schools are parent surrogates. Plato saw plainly this problem of educating children: they should be educated by agencies of the state which have the requisite knowledge of education. Children were to be taken away from parents for purposes of education.

Educational administrators monitor the selection of authorities for their schools. By whatever means teachers are selected the claim that must be protected is their claim to knowledge. No one should be given the power to intervene in the life of another person (a moral enlargement) without requisite achieved authority. Teachers should know what they know and why it is knowledge that passes the apt criteria of excellence.

Authority, guided by criteria of excellence, establishes relevant knowledge and value claims. The point, as has been said many times and in many ways, is not merely to establish authority but to exercise authority in order to remake the world so as to accommodate human purposes. Nowhere can these events be more starkly revealed than in the deliberate effort of educating. School systems that sit boxlike on people like school buildings on the land establish authority but do not exercise it. They "do schooling" but they are not educating. The enterprise of the school system seems merely to keep the system "systematizing"—sorting, processing, fitting, filling, making "inputs into outputs." The business of schooling is business—busy-ness. Educating, when found in schools, is often a threat to schooling, because it reworks the basis of authority and therefore shifts the nature of freedom and mutuality.

Liberty, equality, and fraternity are words of social liberation inspiring the oppressed. In the strange alchemy of public distress, authority is seen as the enemy instead of a strong ally for liberation. Authority so easily slips into authoritarianism. Authoritarianism is the enemy, not authority. Authority, as in authorship, is a responsible claim on the regularities of nature and experience. Authority has its recognized sources and its explicit tests in the antecedents and consequences of authoritative action. We need legitimate authority to establish equality among people. People then need to work to achieve freedom (liberty) and mutuality (fraternity). These achievements are earned by people, not given to them. The mistake of authoritarianism is the assumption of leaders and the expectations of followers that freedom and mutuality can be given out to people, like bread, circuses, and school systems. Educating the people requires close attention to the source of authority, its exercise in daily affairs, and its restructuring for events of the future. Authority is earned power; without it we are powerless.

Mutuality

Of the four key concepts of governance, mutuality is the apex, the achievement devoutly to be wished. The power required to adjudicate claims almost seems to disappear when in the course of human interactions the concept of mutuality is operating. Mutuality as an outcome of educative governance represents a social intimacy, a sharing of joys and responsibilities. When mutuality is achieved, the task of governance ceases.

Not much needs to be said about the fundamental value of mutual accommodation. Where it is experienced it is valued. You scratch my back and I scratch yours and we both feel satisfied. When learners and teachers come together over a curriculum to share meaning, to extend and test meanings, they feel the satisfaction of converting subjectively plausible personal meanings into objectively reasonable shared meanings. The mutuality is a liberation, not an oppressive authority, but self-authorship of scripts of meaning. When we learn to control meaning we learn to govern ourselves. Both meaning and governance are social. The responsibility rests with us, not with some external power. When mutual accommodation occurs through reciprocity of roles and rules, the result is a shared directiveness.

In the early part of this chapter I wrote that if things would just run on their own, then administrators would be out of a job, and now I want to proclaim why that would be a good thing. Governance is an event of governing not limited to administrators. We all govern—teachers, learners, administrators; even the curriculum has a role in governing. If mutuality is achieved, then no administrator is needed because everyone is acting in accord with the shared meaning the situation requires. Many hands make light work; the energies of many are commuted into a sustaining energy for each. Justice is achieved as each claim is satisfied and each claimant understands the relation of one to all. To put something larger than oneself in first place, and the self in second place is for some the meaning of faith. Mutuality, as the apex of concepts of governance, respects this meaning of shared experience. Life without administrators is just as easy as life with them if each person is a governor, responsible with all for shared directiveness.

Let us move to the top of the left side of the V in Figure 5.

Governance is the domain of education where social theories are most relevant. Plato had a right idea about justice: it must be social justice, where the genuine talents of each person find a fit in the ordered relations to every other person. We do not think these days about philosopher-kings governing our society, but Plato's idea can be seen in a modern light. If we think that the philosopher-king was an extremely well educated person, using education wisely to adjudicate the claims of all in the name of justice and order, we can ask ourselves if it is not possible for human beings in general to perform the same role, if *educated.*

Social justice does not demand a class system, of the elite and the masses; or the Greek state's three levels of free persons living on the backs of slaves, or the class system of producing workers versus investment capitalists. Social justice does demand a comprehensive view, a systematic method for adjudicating conflicts, a productive system to generate self and social renewal, and the end of oppressiveness wherever human beings are found. These requirements present a complex set of questions and answers which extend into and go beyond the domain of education. Education is a necessity for the continuity of any social order, baleful or benign, and it is with this fact that educational governance and social theory come together.

Considerations for the Right Side of the Governance V

Administration, in the context of governing educative events, as a practical matter, is a matter of representing, protecting, and encouraging the special claims of each part of the whole of educating activities. Special powers have special claims. Special claims will conflict with other special claims. The administrator is an adjudicator of claims. Under the umbrella notion of social justice, the administrator judges the claims of each in view of the claims of all.

The most significant procedural commitment for the administrator, according to this theory of educating, is to apply the full panoply of conceptual distinctions to the events of educative interest. Each of the chapters in this book presents a relevant conceptual structure. Each of the conceptual distinctions marks a place where a judgment favoring one idea over another can be made. *Every concept is a candidate for conversion to a criterion of judgment.* Every such criterion can be used for settling claims within each area of teaching, curriculum, and learning. For claims between commonplaces there are two general recommendations: one is to look within the area of governance itself, especially the discussion of how an administrator gets a sense of direction; the other major recommendation is to call attention to the whole theory of educating as presented above in Chapter 2.

The key point in settling claims has to be the basic concern of educating. The key value of educating is a release and harnessing of power. That which is of *value* in educating supplies us with the first standard for settling claims. Some claims would be chosen over others because they help students to gain possession of their powers. In a conflict between a teacher wanting to teach reading to elementary school pupils and an administrator wanting teachers to collect milk money from pupils, the conflict must be settled in favor of reading because reading is a primary way human beings come into possession of their powers.

Criteria of excellence derived from curriculum analysis give us one basis for settling competing curricular claims. Whether mathematics should be chosen over history would depend on (1) the specific math or history content and its accessible criteria of excellence, and (2) the extent to which the material can be judged to promote educational value—that is, to help individuals come into possession of their powers, to integrate thinking, feeling and acting, to become self-educating. For the individual person, as a student learning, competing claims should be settled in terms of the extent to which any one claim promotes the integration of thinking, feeling and acting.

Teacher Claims

Each of the key concepts in this theory can be converted into a criterion for judging claims by the teacher, the curriculum, and the student. We are speaking of the *role* of the teacher in making claims, not giving empirical descriptions of individual teachers or groups of teachers. The teacher's role requires that the teacher must claim to *know* something. This knowledge is backed by the appropriate criteria of excellence of that teacher's field of study. So to say that a teacher stakes a claim to knowledge means a claim to concepts, facts, values, and criteria of excellence. Granted a wide range in quality of actual "experts," the role of the teacher requires an expression of authority, of authoritativeness. The teacher should be *an* authority. The administrator has to protect this basic claim of teachers.

Curriculum Claims

If authority is to enter the educative process without authoritarianism, the authority must be of educative materials, not persons or social structures. No mystical or magical properties are to be attributed to material things. The origin and test of the authority of educative materials is twofold: in the way they refer correctly to regularities in events, and in the way they are taken by human beings to make sense of human experience, including criteria of excellence. Curriculum studies are concerned with the relation between these refined primary sources of meaning and the conversion of these sources into educative materials. Chapter 4, above, undertakes the analysis of claims as found in primary sources. We will not repeat that analysis here, but we call attention to the responsibility of educational governance for care with respect to the legitimate claims within the curriculum. The authority is the authority of the record.

It is all too easy to insert one's particular anti-educational bias at this juncture in the educative process. The analysis and organization of educative materials are, after all, complex tasks done by human beings for other humans. Unless we carefully require independent tests (independent of the makers) for our educative materials, social-cultural prejudice, bias, and mystification can be built definitively right into the materials. Politically, the study of curriculum is potent. UNESCO has kept an up-to-date index to educative materials in the various nations it works with, because a change in text often comes before political change.

Student Claims

Like teachers, students have a claim to knowledge. It is a double claim: a claim for what has been achieved by the student (the student's knowledge), and a claim to *need* to know something new.

Take an example from college admissions procedures. Students have a stake in the testing procedures (in the procedures and not merely in the outcome, i.e., to be admitted or not). Standard achievement and aptitude testing methods deny the student any stake in the procedures, prohibit the student from making a contribution to the test, or deny the possibility that either student or test-maker will learn anything from the testing experience. Compare this standard mode of admission to that of a school of music which conducts individual auditions of prospective students as a condition of admission. Here the equity is readily apparent. The student can select from among his or her best pieces those to play for the audition, and the test-givers can learn something about the quality of the student's performance, style, experience, and need. The student learns something as well: the criteria and conditions for admission, choice with respect to instruction needed, and so forth. Thus the music audition is fair because it recognizes the stake the student has in the procedure. The student's stake may be thought of as a claim (approaching a "right") based upon prior achievements and demonstrated abilities in the form of performances of merit.

Viewing the student as claimant is important. What the student can claim is the most important aspect of the student as student. It simultaneously fixes the meaning structure and the responsibility of the student.

Like teachers, students require protection for claims to the freedom *for* learning and their claim for freedom *from* illegitimate interference in learning. Detailed examples of student claims to authority and freedom and how they are and can be protected are fairly commonplace. Equality, with its variations, is a concept of social justice that does need care in analysis. Equality of educational opportunity is a value claim that must be enforced with social power of considerable magnitude. Equality of educational opportunity is the power claim for the students' positive freedom to learn. The door to educative events must be open equally to all. At this point enforced equality and freedom for learning mean the same thing. It is not always the case that conceptual referents for equality and freedom are the same. Of all the claims *for* students which the governor must act to support strongly, the claims to equality of opportunity come first. Let us not deceive ourselves. Social justice requires power. Power corrupts, as we often think, and it also disrupts, and erupts. We cannot avoid "ruption." If we can think clearly about concepts of authority, freedom, and equality, we will not be surprised by events we are supposed to govern.

Educational administration works primarily with four broad concepts: equality, freedom, authority, and mutuality. The effective adjudication of claims requires that the conditions of equality be met first. An educational administrator knows when the task is completed, when conditions of mutuality have been reached as a consequence of the conditions of equality, freedom, and authority having been met.

Further Speculations for the Right Side of the V

The V is a heuristic device used to represent one way to view the structure of knowledge and value claims. Typically, we apply the V to already completed research studied. Scientific research on governance, in the way it is conceived here, does not exist. Perhaps new studies can be initiated and the new conception tested. Lacking sets of completed studies, the V device will be used primarily as a way to suggest the sorts of claims further empirical studies might produce.

Relevant knowledge about educating does exist, of course, and I am assuming that knowledge claims are already known by those interested in governance. The discussion about how an administrator gets a sense of direction indicates some of those procedures and issues. What follows for the right side of the governance V is, frankly, speculative.

Fact. Let us begin by assuming that we know examples of what counts as a clear case of a governing event. We look at those events to make records of them in order to establish the facts. What, exactly, is controlling the meaning that controls the effort? In general we are interested in the events of agreement among people which provide the basis for *decisions.* Decisions are turning points, choices, ways of indicating one sort of acting rather than another. Decisions may be reported as letters, memoranda, contracts, written agreements, documents of happenings. These paper records are deposits and depositories of events of agreement. Decisions are the primary facts of governing.

Data. Grouped facts, which we call data, are collections of decisions that are formulated as regulations, rules, law (of the legal type). A source book of case law would be an example of the data of governance.

Knowledge Claims. What do we know about equality of educational opportunity? What do we know about the legal basis for charting or aborting a school? What do we know about alternative social structures (democracy, socialism, fascism)? The knowledge claims of governance derive from the artifactual regularities of social order. These claims, in general, answer questions about how we secure cooperation among people so that common purposes can be shared.

Value Claims. In governance value claims are answers to questions about worth. Is one way of sharing purposes better than another? Is representative democracy better than participatory democracy? Is an organizational structure that is hierarchical and bureaucratic better than a flat organizational structure? Is collective bargaining a good way to settle salary disputes? In general value claims are called "policy." Not all relevant value claims of governance are formulated as policy, but all policy claims can be seen as instances of value claims. All policy claims concern such questions as "What ought we to do?" For example, "Is this person receiving fair treatment under our policies?" Our policy may be directed at, for example, eradicating sexual discrimination in the work place, and to this extent the policy promotes one value claim over the others.

One speculation about governance and administration which concerns the right side of the V is appropriate here. Most contemporary work in administration concerns the organizational forms within which administrators work. This speculation leads us to a further discussion of organization in relation to governance.

Organization. Does the foregoing discussion of governance have implications for the form of organization appropriate to governance? In general, organizations are social structures which aid or hinder the sharing of meaning such that common purposes can be exercised. Typical bureaucratic, hierarchical structures filter out all of shared experiences except the *decision.* The higher up in the organization one goes, the more the form of information reaching the decision-maker thins out meaning, until a simple yes or no is all that is required of the decision-maker. Of course, there are many variations of yes and no, such as "maybe," "postpone," "buck this back to Jones," "find out who's responsible," and so forth. But in general the buck stops on somebody's desk, and that person decides for or against. The higher up the flow chart, the less the amount of shared meaning. This fact means that such decisions control the meaning that controls the effort.

One of the times this form of governance fails to work, however, is when the effort changes the meaning of the values that govern. It is relatively rare for stellar effort at the lower ranks to have the effect of changing the governing power of the organization. Organizations which *are* open to this possibility are more like what is conceived of here as *mutuality*—my term for identifying events of cooperation which achieve common and shared purposes and experiences.

This key concept of governance suggests certain requirements of organizational form. First, any social structure is good when it becomes possible for its members to experience the feeling of significance of an organizational form which promotes justice and mutuality. In other words, the organizational form should provide structures which permit actions indicated by the key concept of mutuality. The organizational form should have rational consistency between concepts, events, and facts. Second, a social structure should be created that makes evident to all the fact that claims will be settled in terms of educative value. The claimants should know how to press claims, should know the principles of justice which are operating, and as a consequence should be able to grow better educated. Educational organizations that promote educating are in principle good. Third, members should be able to practice using the conceptual distinctions in the whole cluster of concepts: justice, equality, freedom, authority, mutuality. This practice is necessary because members must experience the connection between concepts and criteria. That key concepts become converted into criteria for settling claims is not well understood. Members of the groups should have social forms such that they can experience the sharing and use of concepts and criteria. Events that help us come into the possession of our powers and that give us power over subsequent events are basically educative events. They are liberating in the sense of positive freedom to think, to feel, and to act. They help us come into possession of our world, both social and natural.

An Example. Universities in America are organized in many different ways. A non-American visitor once remarked to me that knowledge is organized in many ways, but in American universities it is organized into semesters. So pervasive has the semester form become that many students and faculty members have no other sense of academic organization. The governing value of universities becomes obscure. The top value supposedly governing is fundamental inquiry that creates new knowledge and tests such knowledge against specific criteria of truth. Yet only a few faculty members and even fewer students comprehend the structure of knowledge and know the various theories of truth. Faculty research works to make claims to knowledge and truth backed by evidence, by procedural rigor and by public test. But by and large these workers only rarely govern their work by explicit reference to tests of meaning, knowledge, and truth. Perhaps the even flow of productive effort should not be interrupted by explicit tests of governing values. Nevertheless, organizational form should exist in such a way that appropriate claims can be settled by appeal to the top values of the organization. Departures (errors) from governing values need to be detected and corrected. University governance should operate to protect, foster, and stimulate educative value.

In the discussion following Figure 5 (both the left side of the V and the right side), the concepts of power and power over have been used. The analysis of these two concepts was intentionally withheld because it requires a prior understanding of all the other major concepts.

Power Over

Look now at Figure 7 with the legend "Power over." Reading the map from the top, we take the overarching problem of governance to be "power over," a power that is restricted by the assumptions of this education theory of voluntary, free, artifactual, and rational phenomena of interest. We are not dealing with oppressive power or with chaos. Some forms of benign anarchy would be acceptable, but the primary emphasis is upon deliberate and deliberated intervention. Governance is power over educative events in a social setting. Power over valid meaning is assumed.

Power as Control over Valid Meaning. In Chapter 2 we discussed the social psychological dimensions of "feeling controlled." We feel controlled by others when they give us their meaning scripts and we are to accept them as our own. Parents, teachers, administrators, or any other persons having power over us tell us how we are supposed to feel. They attribute meaning to our actions. They establish standards for us to achieve. This form of social control is very ancient and very effective.

We need to become more attentive to the various devices an exploitative system uses to control meaning. *Meaning is the key to understanding oppression.* We must learn to write our own scripts of meaning, not merely to accept the homilies and slogans and sayings and symbolic coercions some externalized "they" gave us.

In adult life, culture supplies the meaning of many concepts used to control people. Two classes of concepts are worthy of

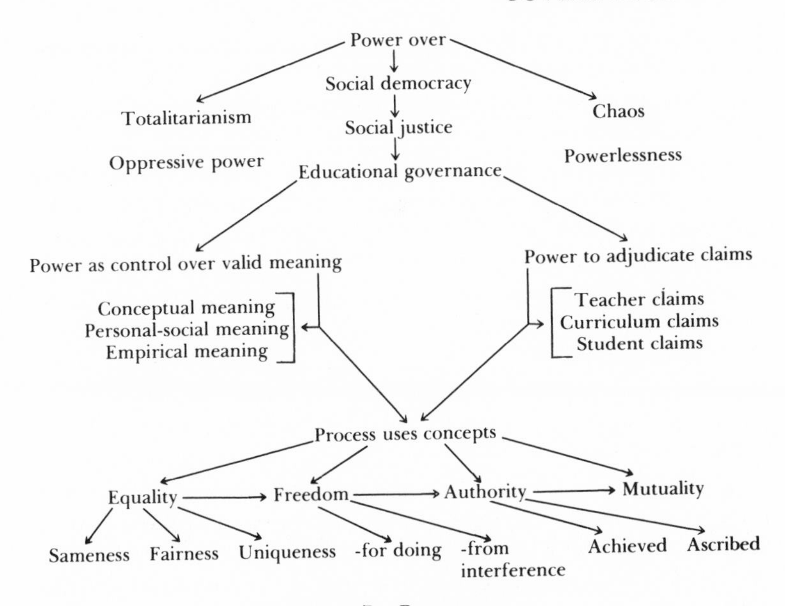

Figure 7. Power over

note: those we use to attribute motivations to others, and those we use to evaluate others. For example, we use phrases like "You want to win, don't you?" "You are really afraid to lose, right?" "Now, you want to cooperate with me, I know." The attribution of the motivation "to win not lose," the success ethic, is perhaps the most common in this culture. The same value, success, is used to evaluate people. A recent cartoon in the *New Yorker* magazine showed a group of well-dressed people at a dinner with one proclaiming, "Money is life's report card." In schools the coin is grades. If a teacher tells a student his performance is ineffective, and if the teacher decides what is and what is not effective, and if the teacher refuses to let the student have any influence over the criteria, then the student will feel highly controlled. Nurse Rachet in *One Flew over the Cuckoo's Nest* is the classic case of an administrator having power over meaning ("You are sick; take your pills") as a way to control the behavior of the inmates. Teachers sometimes feel like controlled inmates because the criteria of success are so elusive. Teachers are expected to suppress their feelings, to be rational, to achieve the (vague) purposes of education, and never to think about losing ("be professional" translates into "be a winner").

Argyris (1975) in a critical review of experimental social psychology, shows how empirical knowledge claims support these views (his model 1). He calls for a shift in the epistemology of research on social behavior to the search for artifactual regularities (his model 2).

For those of us concerned with educating, the quest must be for power over valid meaning. We must learn to write our meaning scripts for ourselves. We must participate in conceiving of the criteria of excellence (rather than success) that help to make sense of nature and human experience. In administration and social governance, control over valid meaning is the most direct control over effort. Figure 7 is an attempt to show the pattern in this chapter. In a social democratic government, both oppressive power and powerlessness are to be avoided. The task of government is to secure cooperation among people so that mutually shared purposes can be achieved. The task of governance in educating is the same.

CHAPTER SEVEN

Self-Educating: Ends and Endings

Begin in midstream, I wrote to begin this book, and I end there as well. In educating, between the beginning and the ending the meaning of experience changes. We end in midstream because educating ourselves is never comprehensively completed, although markers exist in human experience which we perceive as particular ends and endings. Experience itself is an affair of beginnings and endings and where something ends, something else begins. Educating should make us aware of the nature and function of educative events themselves so we can use them to transcend them. When the process of educating brings us through a curriculum to the point where we no longer need a curriculum, a teacher, or governance, then we can be learning on our own, autonomously.

Most human learning does not require deliberate help through the forms of educating. When learning does need help, the theory of educating tells us what to do in educating so persons come into conscious possession of their powers and their world. When we acquire the power to think and feel and act we should use that power. No longer do we require educating.

The end of educating, meaning a stopping place, is always subject-matter specific. We stop further educating in, say, reading, when we come into our powers over words, sentences, text, prose fiction, and so forth. We may continue to learn to read all through life, but we no longer need to be educated in how to read. In another example, when we have done enough work in philosophy such that reflective philosophizing becomes an activity in our life, we can stop further educating in that curriculum. This stopping place does not necessarily mean that one stops learning philosophy. One could perhaps learn more philosophy for all of one's active life. The general point is to distinguish further learning from further educating. Further learning of philosophy can be under a person's own conscious power. But in some new areas, further educating may be needed. Even a well-trained philosopher may need some help from a teacher to open up a new area of study. If I were to take up Chinese philosophy, I could use a teacher to help select the definitive translations, to call attention to special assumptions, to suggest the animating drive of current work—in short, I need someone to crack the code so I can gain access to the doctrines and methods of work.

How does a person (teacher, student) know when educating has come to an end? How does an artist know when a work of art is finished? How does a scientist know when a work of science is finished?

In brief, the answer is when a person has an adequately large conception of the events such that the regularities in those events can be described and judged. Knowing the end is a piece of knowledge, and as such it relates events to concepts and facts as the basis for claims (both knowledge and value claims). If this piece of knowledge is about events of educating, then we will expect to find criteria for judging these events within each of the four commonplaces. Thus, teaching comes to an end with the achievement of shared meaning in the context of educating. Learning ends with the learner's active reorganization of meaning showing that the meaning of experience has been changed for that person. The role of the curriculum ends when the learner no longer needs the curriculum as a means of access to the primary sources of knowledge, when the learner has independent ways to use the world's knowledge. Finally, governance ends with mutuality, when we control meaning to govern ourselves and no other power is needed to bring together teachers, curriculum, and learners. In short, learners know that educating ends when the process of educating lands them on grounds which permit them to transcend the events of educating. The learner now has knowledge about knowledge, has learned about learning, can see when a teacher is and is not needed, and can put all the pieces together under his or her own power. The person has come into possession of power over educative events. From this point on, the person becomes self-educating.

Self-educating is an end of educating. In becoming self-educating we work a change in the role of the four commonplaces. Our teachers may be different, especially as we select teachers ourselves. The curriculum can expand to all bodies of knowledge and we will know to analyze their structures, to search for the criteria of excellence, and to seek alternative explanations of events of central interest. Our knowledge about knowledge can be put to use. Our habitual dispositions to learn will be informed by our knowledge about learning and by our understanding of those prepotent moments of learning when grasping the meaning and feeling the significance come together. Finally, self-educating, like educating, takes place in a social context in which we share experiences with others. We will know how to share educative experiences. The self is never well understood as a cold statue in splendid isolation from the human community. The very possibility of educating depends upon mutuality. No educating occurs in the land of the solipsists because shared experience does not occur there. When educating changes the meaning of human experience, it is human experience and not merely private experience that is changed.

If we grant that educating changes the meaning of experience, we can always ask: changing toward what? If we also grant that through educative experience we make more connections between events, concepts, and facts, we can ask: what makes these increased connections also better? What constitutes the enrichment of experience? Meanings are not entities; they are not the atoms of experience, nor darting molecules of human life; they are not fixed building blocks of a house of intellect. Meanings mark off changes in experience as one thing comes to stand for another in experience. What can happen to meanings?

Let us see. Meanings can become:
clearer, less muddled
extended, increased, multiplied

increased in complexity, differentiation, nuance
capable of attachment to other meanings; more "hooks" extend; bonding occurs
capable of disattachment in contexts in which they occur; they are extractable
richer in ambiguity
full, rounded, settled, complete
systematic
frames of reference
flexible, durable, useful, enduring, satisfying
serviceable in signaling, anticipating, gesturing to the future
other meanings.

As human experience changes to have qualities represented on the above list, we can judge experience has become enriched. There is more to it; it becomes better organized; it leads to new places; we understand more with less. If a person's pattern of organization of meanings shows anything like the variety of the list (and it could be much more extensive), then are we not willing to say that the person's experience has been enriched?

But perhaps it has become *too rich* a mixture. Consider for a moment the common idea of "rich." The frequently heard quip has it that "I've been poor and rich and rich is better."

Which meaning of "rich" do we want to accept? The word "rich" stands for many different things. Obviously, it is possible, in the coinage of ordinary language, to recognize states of being which are "too rich," are too much of the sort of thing they are. We speak of elegance, of elaborate detail in workmanship, or ornateness, of superabundance and conspicuous consumption of the rich. It may be counterintuitive, but I think it is instructive, to think that one can overdo "enrichment" in education. There must be some marker, some cut-off point, between being abundantly educated and being too-richly educated. One of the unusual tasks of evaluation is to make that serious judgment that there has been too much of a good thing. In order to make this judgment, however, we need some way to judge just what a good thing is in education. What might it mean to talk about "richness" or enrichment, without committing the error of eros extended?

Rich in educative value means power to make events happen which are both intrinsically and instrumentally valuable educationally. Educational enrichment of experience means power over events as a consequence of seeing how things are connected, how they fit together, how networks of meaning permit us to extract from one experience meanings to use in another context altogether. *Educational enrichment is the progressive experience of educative significance.* We find endings in experience in which we experience a better integration of feelings, thought, and actions.

Integrated meanings expand our range and we become more autonomous because we are no longer dependent on one small set of meanings. As teachers and the curriculum and the qualities of social life shape our own learning, we come to see our liberation from the necessarily limited beginning sources of our understanding. As we become educated we become liberated from strong external sources of authority and power and become more accepting of our own authority and power, especially the competence we must have to write our own scripts of meaning.

I have noted, along with many other peoople, that writing is rewriting. Whatever writing we produce almost always can be rewritten to make it better. At some point we stop, perhaps turn over our efforts to an editor, and realize that we cannot make it very much better with additional effort. In a sense, educating is like writing in that our early efforts can be improved upon, that we can use help from other people no matter how self-sufficient we feel, and that at some point we must cease. Educating can become reeducating. To say that educating is reeducating suggests several things: that we begin with what we have in present time; that the activities are reflexive (feedback loops abound); that the process has a full course to run but never a final destination; that once we understand educative events through clear cases of educating we will understand what we need to do to make subsequent educative events happen; that we become reflexively aware of what we have, know and value; we develop knowledge about knowledge.

By reflexive review of the processes of art or science or educating we develop categories, commonplaces, and concepts through which we develop criteria to judge these processes. From the study of literary art, we use the commonplace of artist, audience, universe, and work of art, and within each of these we develop appropriate concepts, and from knowledge of these regularities we devise criteria of excellence. The case of science is the same; from critical review of scientific knowledge we develop criteria to judge that knowledge. The studies using the V show how nine or ten elements are related to make the structure of knowledge. We need not repeat that analysis here. Suffice it to claim that what is produced from this reflexive scrutiny are the procedures and standards of *evaluation*. Knowing how to judge the places where processes end is knowledge supporting evaluation. Evaluation is built in as concepts of events become converted to criteria for judging the regularities of those events. In the analysis of clear cases we use criteria, and from such analysis we devise new criteria useful in judging new cases. Occasionally, criteria from outside are brought in and their meaning established through their use on exemplary cases.

In this book, for example, criteria from outside of education have been brought in to help examine cases and events of educating. I have drawn from three sources of ideas—philosophy, science, and common sense. Citing these sources would not establish the value or authority of the ideas. It will seem to some readers that I have scanted sources and not respected the authorities. I could detail which philosophers I read and recovered from, which scientific claims shook the scales from my eyes. I could recount some of the special experiences I have had as a teacher, a curriculum-writer, a learner, and an administrator, which placed me in the cauldron of educative events. In some places I have cited my sources but, for several reasons, I have not felt it important to do so. One reason is that I want the construction of claims in this book to be a tub that stands on its own bottom insofar as that is possible. My working with these ideas has led me to feel their power in interaction with students and other teachers. I like the way one idea plays off another and leads to a third idea. Insofar as there is a coherent vision here, I have wanted to give it expression in its own terms. A second reason for scanting authorities is most immodest, yet it is basic to my sense of the authority of a teacher. A teacher should be *an* authority. One among many, yes, but still *one*. I realize all too well sometimes the limits of my authority. I will take my lumps. Sources are important, yes, but consequences seem to me to be a better test of the meaning and truth of ideas than any detailing of their origin. *Authority derives from the continual testing of claims for their utility in changing the meaning of human experience.* Merely citing authorities is never conclusive. It is doubtful that any philosopher ever held sway over the minds of other people except when some quality of his thought made sense of their understanding of nature and human experience.

In judging the end of educating, it may be helpful to make a distinction between ends and aims. An end of educating is self-educating; an aim of educating is to change the meaning of an experience. That is our focus as educators: to aim at those qualities of present experience which are in themselves educative, which permit educating to happen.

Educative happenings focus on sharing meaning in present time. If I were a playwright perhaps I could sketch better what I mean about educating in present time. Think of a drama. As we watch the unfolding of the play we observe how events change and how changes in events lead us on to a different meaning. For example, we may not have noticed explicitly the shotgun hanging on the wall in the first act, but we get its meaning when it becomes the murder weapon in the second act. In a play of a love triangle, the first appearance of the third party changes the meaning of the relation between the original pair. Each actor, each part, contributes to changes in meaning of events. In the art of the playwright, beginnings and endings are qualities of events transformed by what happens in between. The playwright uses words, of course, to compose the script, but the script is more than words; it is a structure of actions. Events are not all words; educating is not all cognitive meaning. In a play the dancers must perform their choreographed actions, the music must be heard, the silences must be endured. In self-educating we each of us *act.* Events of such actions are necessary for educating. Of all the promising possibilities for combatting boredom in school and life, my first choice would be to capture an event sense of educating.

Educating and miseducating are universal human phenomena.

They are the ways that one generation of human beings shapes the beliefs, behaviors, and actions of subsequent generations. Like all human experience, the events of educating are both stable and precarious. They are regular and spontaneous, durable and ephemeral, alloyable, miscible, changeable. Educative events are in some ways simple and direct and every human being can upon some reflection recall the experience of true educative happenings of sharing meaning and expanding experience. Yet these educative events are so easily contaminated and complicated by other events as to be functionally lost. Like loving, educating is a human good and where experienced it is valued. Like loving, it gets corrupted into serving many other purposes. Like loving, it can be absent for long periods of time but never forever.

Bibliography

Argyris, Chris. 1975. "Dangers in Applying Results from Experimental Social Psychology," *American Psychologist,* 30, 469–485.

Argyris, Chris, and Cyert, Richard M. 1980. *Leadership in the 80's: Essays on Higher Education.* Cambridge, Mass.: Institute for Educational Management, Harvard University.

Ausubel, D., Novak, J. D., and Hanesian, H. 1978. *Educational Psychology: A Cognitive View.* New York: Holt, Rinehart & Winston.

Bateson, Gregory. 1979. *Mind and Nature.* New York: Dutton.

Black, Max. 1962. "Metaphor," in *Models and Metaphors.* Ithaca: Cornell University Press.

Black, Max. 1977. "More About Metaphor," *Dialectica,* Vol. 31: 3–4, 432-57.

Dewey, John. 1916. *Democracy and Education.* New York: Macmillan.

Dewey, John. 1938. *Logic, the Theory of Inquiry.* New York: Henry Holt.

Dewey, John. 1958. *Art as Experience.* New York: Capricorn.

Dewey, John. 1959. *Experience and Nature.* New York: Dover.

Donaldson, Margaret. 1978. *Children's Minds.* Glasgow: Collins.

Fenstermacher, Gary. 1979. "A Philosophical Consideration of Recent Research on Teacher Effectiveness," *Review of Research in Education.* Itasca, Ill.: F. E. Peacock.

Flanagan, John C. 1979. *Perspectives on Improving Education.* American Institute of Research.

Fromm, Erich. 1970. *The Art of Loving.* New York: Bantam.

Gowin, D. Bob. 1961. "Teaching, Learning and Thirdness," *Studies in Philosophy of Education,* Vol. 1:3, 87-113.

Gowin, D. Bob. 1963. "Can Educational Theory Guide Practice?" *Educational Theory,* 12, 6-12.

Gowin, D. Bob. 1970. "The Structure of Knowledge," *Educational Theory,* Vol. 20:4, 319–28.

Gowin, D. Bob. 1975. "Teaching as Making Sense of What is Known," in *The Philosophy of Open Education,* David Nyberg, ed. London and Boston: Routledge & Kegan Paul. Pp. 79–88.

Gowin, D. Bob, Mutkoski, Patricia, and Novak, Joseph. 1981. *Epistemology, Education and Research: A Ten Year Review at Cornell University.* Unpublished manuscript.

Green, Thomas. 1971. *The Activities of Teaching.* New York: McGraw-Hill.

Green, Thomas. 1980. *Predicting the Behavior of the Educational System.* Syracuse: Syracuse University Press.

Jackson, Philip W. 1968. *The Teacher and the Machine.* Pittsburgh: University of Pittsburgh Press.

James, William. 1950. *The Principles of Psychology.* New York: Dover.

Jencks, Christopher, et al. 1979. *The Determinants of Economic Success in America.* New York: Basic Books.

Matthews, Gareth B. 1980. *Philosophy and the Young Child.* Cambridge, Mass.: Harvard University Press.

Millman, Jason, and Gowin, D. Bob. 1974. *Appraising Educational Research.* Englewood Cliffs, N.J.: Prentice-Hall.

Nakosteen, Mehdi. 1965. *The History and Philosophy of Education.* New York: Ronald Press.

Northrup, F. S. C. 1957. "Ethical Relativisim in the Light of Recent Legal Science," in *American Philosophers at Work,* S. Hook, ed. New York: Criterion.

Novak, Joseph D. 1977. *A Theory of Education.* Ithaca: Cornell University Press.

Novak, Joseph D. 1981. *The Use of Concept Mapping and Gowin's "V" Mapping Instructional Strategies in Junior High School Science: The Cornell University "Learning How to Learn" Project.* Unpublished report.

Peirce, Charles. 1878. "How to Make Your Ideas Clear," *The Popular Science Monthly.*

Peirce, Charles. 1958. *Values in a Universe of Chance.* P. P. Wiener, ed. Garden City, N.Y.: Doubleday Anchor.

Rapaport, A. 1954. *Operational Philosophy.* New York: Harper.

Richards, I. A. 1936. "Metaphor," Lecture V of *The Philosophy of Rhetoric.* Oxford: Oxford University Press.

Robinson, Richard. 1950. *Definition.* Oxford: Clarendon Press.

Scheffler, I. 1960. *The Language of Education.* Springfield, Ill.: C. C. Thomas.

Schwab, Joseph J. 1978. *Science, Curriculum, and Liberal Education.* Ian Westbury and Neil J. Wilkof, eds. Chicago: University of Chicago Press.

Scriven, Michael. 1976. *Reasoning.* New York: McGraw-Hill.

Terkel, Louis. 1979. *Working.* New York: Avon.

Toulmin, S. 1972. *Human Understanding,* Vol. 1. Princeton: Princeton University Press.

Ulich, Robert. 1948. *3,000 Years of Educational Wisdom.* Cambridge, Mass.: Harvard University Press.

Wilson, Woodrow. 1887. "The Study of Administration," *Political Science Quarterly,* 2, 210.

Index

ABC materials: derived from bodies of knowledge, 54; related to teaching, 77
Administrator: as executive, 159-61; as group process leader, 161-63; and importance of concepts, 169-70; and role theory, 166-69; sense of direction, 157-69; as social scientist, 163-69
Advance organizers, 114
Aims, 201
Argyris, Chris, 194
Artifactual phenomena of interest, 26-28
Artifactual regularities, 27, 157
Attention, 51
Ausubel, David, 143
Authoritarianism, 181
Authority: ascribed vs. achieved, 181; and curriculum, 89; in governance, 181-83; and liberty, fraternity, equality, 182-83; mutuality, 183-84; and power, 181; of the record, 114, 186; source of, 201

Bateson, Gregory, 149
Behavior, as action with meaning, 41
Behavioral science, critique of in administration, 163-65
Behaviorist view: of educating, 37-38; of teaching, 64
Black, Max, 145-46

Change: concept of, in educating, 37-39; in meaning of experience, 37
Choice, 51
Claiming, as learning, 131
Classical views: of educating, 39; of teaching, 64-66
Classroom management, 56-57
College admission procedures, students' stake in, 187
Commonplaces of educating, 25
Competing claims: of curriculum, students, and teachers, 186-87
Conceiving, defined, 128
Concentration, in studying, 36-37
Concept analysis, and research, 31
Concept maps: of educating, 94; explained, 93-95; and learning, 124; of power, 193
Concepts: converted to criteria, 200; defining of, 29-30; learning through metaphors, 145; and logical operators, 97; in research, 30; of teaching, 73; and words, 97
Conceptual structures, in curriculum, 92
Conceptualizing, defined, 128
Consensus, and governance, 162-63
Construction of meaning: and governance, 155; and power, 155; and social setting, 155
Constructs, and concepts, 96
Context of inquiry, and meaning, 102
Controlling meaning: and governance, 153-56; and power over events, 155
Cooperation, and governance, 156-57

Criteria of excellence: and curriculum, 54, 112, 116-17; development of, 199, 200; diverse forms, 47; for educating, 121; and governance, 154, 185; and intelligence, 47; in literary works, 86; in science, 85; student's use of, 76-77; teachers' use of, 77-78
Criteria of judgment, 185
Criticizing, as learning, 129
Culture: and governance, 162; patterns of, 26-27
Curriculum: and criteria of excellence, 54; definitions of, 84-85, 107-9; as governance, 108-11; as learning, 108-11; as records of events, 113; roles of educative materials in, 112-15; steps in making, 116-20; and structure of knowledge, 84-85; as teaching, 108-11
Curriculum inquiry, 119-121; method, 115

Data, as transformed facts, 29, 101
Decisions, 189
Definitions, concept and operational, 95
Democratic leadership, as governance, 161-63
Dewey, John: five steps, 29; growth, 45; logic, 115
Disciplined criticism (method of study), 32
Donaldson, Margaret, 23
Drill and exercise, in studying, 142

Educating: changing the meaning of human experience, 39-43; clear cases of, 24; concept map of, 94; sense of direction in, 35-36; significant connection making, 46; working definition of, 35-36
Educational value, 45-47
Educative dyads, 74-77
Educative events: artifactual, 76; key event, 28; materials as guides to, 55
Educative materials, 54-56
Ending: of curriculum, 196; of governance, 196; of learning, 196; of teaching, 196
Enrichment: educational, 199; of experience, 197
Episodic nature of teaching, 79
Epistemology, 28; outcome of knowledge defined, 87-88
Equality: applied to research, policy and practice, 179; contest analogy, 175-76; fairness, 174-75; feast analogy, 177-78; hospital analogy, 176-77; logical analysis of, 171-75; related to equality of, 180; sameness, 172-74; uniqueness and identity, 171-72
Errors, as part of teaching and learning, 75
Ethics, and governance, 56-57, 170
Evaluation, 198, 200
Event: and epistemology, 28; key educative, 28
Excellence, concepts of, 36
Explanation: and causal generalization, 103; and reasons, 104

Facts: and data, 101; defined, 100-101; learning facts, 146-147; and methods, 99; ordering, 30; records of events, 28
Factual judgments, 30
Feelings: as existential reality, 48; and learning, 132-33
Felt significance: as value, 43
Fenstermacher, Gary, 150
Formal education: liberation, 35; intervention, 35
Freedom: and choice, 51; and excellence, 36; generating new meanings, 50; in governance, 180-81; and thought, 50
Freud, Sigmund, 92
Fromm, Erich: *Art of Loving,* 50; separation as problem of human existence, 44-45
Frost, Robert, 158

Generalization, defined, 103
Governance: and criteria fo excellence, 154; as controlling meaning, 56; definition, 57; formula of, 154; and meaning theory, 158-69; and power, 153; as social control, 56-60; telling questions of, 156-57; validating claims, sharing meaning, 155
Grasping meaning: examples of, 41;

Grasping meaning (*cont.*)
and feeling significance, 43; and learning, 41, 125
Green, Thomas F., 136, 164

Heuristic teaching, 67-71
Hoffer, Eric, 90
Human nature, 49-50

Imagining, as learning, 129
Individualism, critique of, 160
Indoctrination, defined, 72
Intelligence, as habitual disposition, 47
Interpretation, in research, 31
Intervention: and liberation, 35-36; and teaching, 53
Is and *ought*, 165-69

Jackson, Philip, 79
James, William, 51

Knowing, and learning, 101
Knowledge about knowledge, 24, 27, 149; deliberate construction, 27
Knowledge claims, 101-2

Leaky pail theory of meaning, 169
Learner: as causal agent, 133-36; prior knowledge of, 124; and responsibility of, 133-34; self-interest of, 48-49
Learning: absence of laws of, 122-23; common sense view of, 122; as cultural artifact, 123; and curriculum, 144; definition, 124-25; and educating, 124; and governance, 148; and language, 123; and meaning, 41; as questioning and answering, 126-32; and responsibility, 41; and studying, 136; and teaching, 150
Learning about learning, 24
Lecturing: and training, 66-67

Marx, Karl, 92
Mastery, in studying, 137-39
Matthews, Gareth, 23
Meaning: and behavior, 41; changes in, 197-98; construction of, 40-41; definition of, 40; and feelings, 42; integrated, 199
Mendel, Gregor, 92

Metaphor, 145
Method: defined, 98; and facts, 99; learning a method, 147; and techniques, 99
Millman-Gowin study, and curriculum inquiry, 116-20
Miseducating, 201-2

Nakosteen, Mehdi, 32
Northrup, F. S. C., 165-66
Novak, Joseph, 121, 143

Oppression: breaking the cycle of, 58-59; internalized, 57-60; key to, 192; schoolism, 57
Organization, requirements for form of, 19-92

Patience: in studying, 141-42
Peirce, Charles, 51
Persuasive communication, distinguished from teaching, 71
Phenomena of interest: artifactual, 26-28; self-reflexive, 23; of a theory of educating, 28
Philosophizing, as learning, 129
Philosophy of education, and research, 31
Policy: value claims in governance, 189-90
Power: and controlling meaning, 153-56; and events, 187-88; and freedom, 187-88; and governance, 153; possession of, 40; source of student's, 81
Power over, 192-94
Practice, in studying, 141
Principles, making of as learning, 128
Process of educating, 36-37
Progressive teaching: and curriculum, 114-15; defined, 82-83

Q-5 (method of analysis), 88
Questioning-and-answering, as learning, 126-32

Rapaport, Anatol, 96
Recording, as learning, 130-31
Records of events, and curriculum, 113
Reeducating, defined, 199
Reliability, 29

Research: aim of, 27; artifactual regularities in, 27; basic requirements of, 29-32; validity of, 29
Responsibility, and students, 148; and teachers, 53
Richards, I. A., 145, 146
Robinson, Richard, 95
Rogers, Carl, 64
Routines, in studying, 139-40

Self-educating, 197
Sense of the whole, in studying, 140-41
Sharing meanings: and definition of teaching, 62; and governance, 155; makes educating possible, 40
Skinner, B. F., 64
Social context, 25
Social control, principles of, 155
Social justice: and governance, 56, 184; principle of, 56
Social meaning, shared experience, 40
Structure of knowledge, defined, 87-88
"Studenting," need for, 63
Studies, traditions of, (ideological, practical, scientific), 32
"Studyability," of curriculum, 117-18
Studying, concepts of, 136-42
Studying educating: artifactual phenomena, 26-28; difficulties in, self-reflexive phenomena of interest, 23-25; embedded familiarity, 25-26
Symbols, and concepts, 40

Teachers: authority, 63; and intervention, 53-54; responsibilities, 53
Teaching: as an art, 151; concepts of, 73-80; defined, 62; efficient cause, 52; as episodic, 79-80; heuristic, 67-71; and learner's responsibilities, 63; as shared meaning, 62-63, as triadic, 73-78
Telling questions: defined, 90-91; of governance, 155-57
Theorizing, as learning, 129
Theory: concept of, 26; of educating, 28; as guide to action, 165-69; role of in research, 34
Thinking, feeling, and acting, 46, 48
Time, as unit in educating, 37
Toulmin, Stephen, 24
Training: defined, 72; and instruction, 66
Transforming, as learning, 131

Ulich, Robert, 32
Understanding, linkages in, 104-5

The V: explained, 28-29, 107; governance, 157; learning, 127; and research, 34
Value: defined, 44-47; utility for educating, 41
Value claims, 105-6

Wilson, Woodrow, 159

XYZ materials: bodies of knowledge, 54; related to teaching, 77

EDUCATING

Designed by Richard E. Rosenbaum.
Composed by The Composing Room of Michigan, Inc.
in 10 point Baskerville V.I.P., 2 points leaded,
with display lines in Baskerville.
Printed offset by Thomson/Shore, Inc. on
Warren's Number 66 Antique Offset, 50 pound basis.
Bound by John H. Dekker & Sons, Inc.
in Holliston book cloth.

Library of Congress Cataloging in Publication Data

Gowin, D. B.
Educating.

Bibliography: p.
Includes index.
1. Teaching. 2. Self-culture. I. Title.
LB1025.2.G627 370 81-66646
ISBN 0-8014-1418-0 AACR